Drawing and Painting

Series listing

Mollie Davies: *Movement and Dance in Early Childhood*
2nd edition 2003
John Matthews: *Drawing and Painting: Children and Visual Representation*
2nd edition 2003
Marian Whitehead: *Developing Language and Literacy with Young Children*
2nd edition 2002
Rosemary Roberts: *Self-esteem and Early Learning* 2nd edition 2002
Cath Arnold: *Child Development and Learning 2–5 – Georgia's Story* 1999
Pat Gura: *Resources for Early Learning* 1997
Chris Pascal and Tony Bertram: *Effective Early Learning – case studies in
   improvement* 1997

All titles are available from Paul Chapman Publishing
http://www/paulchapmanpublishing.co.uk

The 0–8 Series

The 0–8 Series edited by Professor Tina Bruce, deals with essential themes in early childhood which concern practitioners, parents and children. In a practical and accessible way, the series sets out a holistic approach to work with young children, families and their communities. It is evidence based, drawing on theory and research. The books are designed for use by early years practitioners, and those on professional development courses, and initial teacher education courses covering the age-range 0–8.

Drawing and Painting

Children and Visual Representation

Second Edition

John Matthews

P·C·P

Paul Chapman
Publishing

Paul Chapman Publishing
A SAGE Publications Company
6 Bonhill Street
London EC2A 4PU

SAGE Publications Inc
2455 Teller Road
Thousand Oaks, California 91320

SAGE Publications India Pvt Ltd
B-42, Panchsheel Enclave
Post Box 4109
New Delhi 1 100 017

Library of Congress Control Number: 200210727

A catalogue record for this book is available from the
British Library

ISBN 0 7619 4785 X
ISBN 0 7619 4786 8 (pbk)

Typeset by Dorwyn Ltd, Rowlands Castle, Hants
Printed in Great Britain by The Cromwell Press, Trowbridge

Note: In this book I have mostly used the pronouns 'her', 'hers' for children in general, unless I
am referring to a particular, male individual. Although (sadly) the vast majority of early
childhood educators are women, I have used the pronoun 'him' and 'his' when referring to
the teacher in general. I will also be obliged to use the terms, 'teaching, teacher, learning,
learner', although I no longer believe in such things. I will be obliged to refer to other
imaginary entities like 'subjects' and 'disciplines'. The readers should bear in mind that these
are convenient but artificial labels for aspects of processes we do not understand. I will also be
forced to make a distinction between something called 'development' and something called
'learning', although, I believe, no such distinction exists.

This edition is dedicated to Joseph Ng

'Children draw for fun.' (Georges Luquet, 1923, p.1)

Contents

Series Preface

The 0–8 Series has stood the test of time, maintaining a central place among early childhood texts. Practitioners have appreciated the books because, while very practical, the series presents a holistic approach to work with young children, which values close partnership with families and their communities. It is evidence based, drawing on theory and research in an accessible way.

The 0–8 Series, now being revised and updated, continues to deal with the themes of early childhood which have always been of concern and interest to parents, practitioners and the children themselves. The voice of the child has, since 1989, been under threat in education. Each author has made an important contribution in their field of expertise, using this within a sound background of child development and practical experience with children, families, communities, schools and other early childhood settings. The series consistently gives a central place to the interests and needs of children, emphasising the relationship between child development and the socio-cultural learning with which biological and brain development is inextricably linked. The voice of the child is once again being understood as being important if children are to develop and learn effectively, and if adults helping them to learn (teaching them) are to be effective in their work.

The basic processes of communication, movement, play, self-esteem and understanding of self and others, as well as the symbolic layerings in development (leading to dances, reading, writing, mathematical and musical notations, drawing, model-making) never cease to fascinate those who love and spend time with children. Some of the books in this series focus on these processes of development and learning, by looking at children and their contexts in a general way, giving examples as they go. Other books take a look at particular aspects of individual children and the community. Some emphasise the importance of rich physical and cultural provision and careful consideration of the environment indoors and outdoors and the way that adults work with children.

As Series Editor I am delighted to reintroduce the 0–8 Series to a new readership. The re-launched series enters a more favourable climate than the original series, which survived (and flourished) in a hostile climate of literacy hours for four-year-olds, adult-led learning, and a lack of valuing diversity, multi-lingualism, imagination and creativity. This revised and updated 0–8 Series will inform, support and inspire the next generation of early childhood practitioners in the important work they do, in a climate which will encourage rather than undermine.

I look forward to seeing the impact of the 0–8 Series on the next decade.

Professor Tina Bruce
London Metropolitan University
October 2001

Preface

Dr John Matthews has expanded the popular first edition of his book to share with readers the work he has done in Singapore. He has also made enriching reference to his grandchildren and their artistic and expressive development.

The book resonates with respect for the creativity of children, and gives practical help to those living with and working with babies and young children. His work is powerfully underpinned with evidence from the research literature. He shows great courage in holding steadfastly to an approach to teaching art which draws on evidence available, and which is supported with clusters of theories that do not contradict each other. He also gives the views of those who take a different stance.

His work has earned him an international reputation as a scholar in his field, and yet he has never lost touch with his practical work with children. His enjoyment of working with them in home or early years settings beams out on every page, as he writes with obvious fascination for the way children develop in their visual representations, especially through mark-making.

The book gives a 'can do' message to practitioners and those training them. Although he shows us Ben's paintings and drawings, which are exceptional in every aspect, he also shows us how we can help every child in every cultural context to develop the ability to represent in paint, drawings or constructions, and so enrich thoughts, ideas, imagination, feelings and relationships, as well as technical prowess.

The first edition was a much loved text for many practitioners. The second edition, with its cross-cultural and cross-generation perspectives, looks likely to offer those in the field of early childhood training and practice another gem.

Tina Bruce, Series Editor
September 2002

Acknowledgements

The debts to Piaget, Luquet, Chris Athey, Alan Costall, John Willats, Colwyn Trevarthen, Esther Thelen and Linda Smith are obvious. The encouragement of Brent Wilson, Elliot Eisner, Anna Kindler and Dennis Atkinson has been important to me. I also owe a great deal to Dennie Wolf, Rebecca Chan and the late, great, Nancy Smith. My thanks, of course, to Ben, Joel and Hannah Matthews.

I am also grateful for the support of my colleagues in Visual and Performing Arts, National Institute of Education, Nanyang Technological University, Singapore, and to Dr Li Lian Chang and Dr Ken Ung.

I would like to especially acknowledge the help of Linda Matthews. Most of my better days came from her.

Introduction

This book shows how young children's drawings and paintings begin and develop, and why their early visual representations and expressions are important – namely because, when they *represent* anything (using a mark, a shape, an action or an object) *they make something stand for something else*, and through *expression* (in speech, action or images) *they show emotion*. They also use visual media to produce and investigate lines, shapes and colours in a process which is related to other intellectual domains, for example, language, logic and mathematics. Children use anything they can get their hands on to form the beginnings of symbolic thought (Kress, 1997). Drawing especially helps the child's understanding of symbols, and signs and representation, understanding which will become crucial in her encounters with symbol and sign systems in home and school, and in the expanded world of literacy she will enter when she leaves school. This means that, in actions they can make with their own bodies, and in actions they can perform upon objects and media, but perhaps especially with drawing and painting media, children learn how to form representations, symbols and signs. This forms the basis for all thinking. If you think this through, this means that, far from being at the periphery of education, what adults call 'children's art' has a central role to play in cognitive development. To think otherwise is a 'fundamental misconception' (Eisner, 1997).

In contemporary art, drawing can take many forms, some of which produce no mark or trace. However, to keep things simple, in this book drawing is defined as a predominantly linear way of defining shapes and events. Often, but not necessarily, drawing actions leave a trail or visible line. Painting uses coloured pigment, in patches of surface colour, to describe areas. In practice, however, what we think of as drawing and painting naturally overlap. Additionally, although painting and drawing require particular skills, these activities are linked to a whole range of actions children make to express their feelings and represent their worlds. Although drawings and paintings represent the main focus of the book, I feel it is important to show how these link with the growth of representation as a whole. Therefore, I will also discuss how children use a range of actions, materials and media through which to express their feeling and represent their realities.

Many people's inherited wisdom about children's development in the visual arts derives from a traditional 'stage' theory of development. This stage theory describes development in terms of a gradual progression from supposedly inferior ways of drawing, starting from meaningless 'scribbling', through successively superior 'stages' until children finally resolve the supposed 'errors' in their drawing and are at last able to produce 'correct' representations. What is deemed 'correct' varies from time to time and from place to place, but one very influential theory supposes the end point of development to be a form of 'visually realistic' picture. Some psychologists look at children's drawings and paintings to see how 'visually realistic' they are, which means that most children's drawings are thought to be full of mistakes. Moreover, according to this approach, some of children's earliest drawings are not considered drawings at all. These authors write about what they think is wrong with the ways children make drawings and think of drawing development as the 'stages' through which children must pass before they are able to produce 'visually realistic' pictures (Piaget and Inhelder, 1956; Lowenfeld and Brittain, 1970). To readers who are acquainted with modern and contemporary art, it might seem old-fashioned and anomalous that children's development in visual art be measured against a 'visually realistic' exemplar, yet the ghost of this model continues to haunt cognitive psychology and education. Transported originally from European art practice, this end point (in one guise or another) is assumed by the education systems worldwide. Even the goal of today's electronic media is often conceived of in just the same way; as a completely faithful copy of reality – a 'virtual reality'.

Of course, visual realism is not the only goal assumed for art education, but whatever representational and expressive expectations are required of children, they all are concerned with 'civilising' children into a 'correct' representation of reality, whether this be forcing early twentieth-century Native American boys to draw 'still-life' drawings (Wilson, 1997), or the preparation of child slaves for today's electronic sweatshops.

It turns out that 'visual realism' is not so easy to define, and we will return to this problem later. At this point, suffice it to say that I do not favour the view that young children only scribble, or produce deficient drawings until they can produce visually realistic pictures or some other form of supposedly 'correct' representation. This makes the mistake of comparing children's drawings with one particular type of picture made by artists and other adults. By doing this, a great misunderstanding is made of children's art and its meaning and significance is lost, to the detriment of children's intellectual and emotional development.

Even though I am an artist who loves art, and believes that children are sometimes truly engaged at an aesthetic level, dealing with concerns which are essentially similar to those of many artists, I have mostly avoided the word 'art'. This is partly because children use a wide variety of materials, actions and objects for representation and expression. In fact, they use anything they can get their hands on for the purposes of expression and representation. But the main reason for avoiding the term 'art' has to do with the child's developing conceptions. While it is true that some contemporary artists also use a wide variety of media, some of which is unconventional, and while they often address issues beyond those of pre-modern art and 'modern' art, nevertheless, children's intentions, and the understandings they form when they use different media, are not captured by *any* adult definition of art.

At first glance, the beginnings of children's representation and expression look trivial, consisting of apparently meaningless actions – twirling, running, jumping up and down, shouting and singing, apparently aimlessly 'messing around' with objects or speech and song. With some important exceptions (Wolf and Fucigna, 1983; Athey, 1990; Matthews, 1994; 1999) most researchers regard these as irrelevant to children's drawing and painting (and people generally do not see these as important to a child's education). Yet, later on, we will see how actions, in themselves, are important. We will see that movement itself is a fundamental form of perception (Thelen and Smith, 1994; Thelen et al., 2000; Allott, 2001).

Even if we narrow our focus to drawing itself, as defined solely in terms of making lines on paper, we still encounter a great deal of misunderstanding. At present there is a downplaying of children's spontaneous drawing. This is the kind of drawing children produce, with great intensity, by and for themselves; drawing which serves their own intentions, and through which they understand the world. Such drawing is essential to children's intellectual and emotional development, yet it is seriously misunderstood and damaged (Matthews, 2001a). Over the last 20 years or so, we have seen the systematic devaluing of children's spontaneous drawing (along with most, if not all, other aspects of children's unsupervised activities and those unlegislated in curricula documents). In many contemporary curricula, including that of England, children do not often get an opportunity to draw freely. It is even becoming difficult to find spontaneous drawings in schools – drawings which have escaped the heavy hand of ill-informed curricular guidance. This is not because children do not produce spontaneous drawings – they continue to generate them with gusto; nor because all teachers dislike them. It is because such drawings, along with other spontaneously generated art forms, and indeed all forms of unsupervised, yet developmentally significant, representational and expressive activity vital to the intellectual and emotional growth of young children, are systematically suppressed by contemporary educational systems.

The school curriculum has been traditionally conceptualised as a set of discrete 'subjects', revolving around a central 'core' of mathematics, science and the country's language. These 'subjects', including 'art', are thought of as 'bodies of knowledge' to be 'delivered' to passive recipients. Given this conceptualisation, the subject 'art', in most educational systems, has a peculiarly limited role to play, based on a profound misunderstanding about its true nature and significance in human development. If young children do get a chance to do some drawing, then this is either out of school or else in a set 'art lesson' following the requirements of Art curricula.

Nowadays, children's art has to be seen to fulfil an educational purpose of a peculiarly limited kind. There is an intolerance of children's spontaneous art, or indeed of any representational or expressive actions, while, at the same time, an encouragement of overt teaching involving an active interference, on the part of teachers, with children's development. However 'flexible' and sensible-sounding the National Curriculum might appear at first glance, the assumption behind it is that the art of young children is a deficient forerunner of superior modes of imagery into which the child must be hurriedly inducted. Put simply, the notion behind the design of the National Curriculum is that children's art, albeit charming to some adults, is unquestionably 'wrong' and in need of 'correction'. In much contemporary art education (so-called) there is a tendency, from early years education onward, to overtly train children in techniques towards end points pre-envisaged in the minds of teachers – or, more precisely, in the minds of curriculum designers working toward government directives.

This book explains the meaning and significance of children's drawings and art forms, and how teachers can support its development in the arts. The book will also explain why, conversely, some approaches to the interpretation and teaching of 'art' are destructive to development.

The focus of this book is upon children's spontaneous drawing; the 'art' that children do by themselves and for themselves. This is not to say that I will be arguing for a laissez-faire approach, in which children are left completely to their own devices. On the contrary, this book will argue for the need of adult interaction and support for early representation and expression, but it will also argue that this support be of a special and subtle kind. I am going to argue that provision for children's early representation should be based upon a knowledge of the developmental significance of children's spontaneous use and organisation of visual media.

The first edition of this book derived from original, longitudinal studies I made of my own three children, Benjamin, Joel and Hannah. I studied my children from birth until they were teenagers. These children were privileged in the sense of having access to art materials and parents who are skilled and interested in drawing and painting as well as knowledgeable about child development. Linda and I helped the children and discussed their drawings and paintings with them.

All three children are now grown up and are accomplished artists. Hannah is currently studying photography. She also plays the flute very well and she is a good dancer. In retrospect, I can see the dawning of these interests in her earliest acts of expression and representation. Joel is now a successful manager of a market, a task which involves creative decision-making. He also plays lead guitar in the rock band, the Arther King Band. Perhaps an unanticipated consequence of Linda's and my own support for his early symbolisation, is Joel's own skills in parenting and childcare. Possibly, he developed these skills through the interactions of Linda and myself with him. I write 'possibly', for although I think that Linda was, and is, an exemplary parent, I cannot claim the same for myself. If the truth be told, Joel is a better father to his children than I ever was to him.

Benjamin had a brain tumour at age fifteen years, recovered from it, continued to produce very good art, read History at Oxford University and is now a successful performance artist in Singapore. (Like many artists, he makes good money too.) Again, in retrospect, I can see the seeds of humour in his early child plays and comedy sketches he performed with his brother, Joel. I did not recognise this as 'theatre' at the time.

I am very proud of them all.

In this, the second edition of the book, I again focus on Ben's development in drawing. The reason for this is that he, especially, used drawing continuously throughout his childhood and adolescence as a way of making meaning. His skills in drawing were apparent in drawings from the age of two and a half years, if not before, and throughout infancy and childhood he drew nearly every day, producing thousands of drawings as well as hundreds of sculptures. As I mentioned above, with his younger brother, Joel, he also produced some extremely funny and entertaining theatre. Focusing upon Ben's work allows us the unusual opportunity of a glimpse into a detailed developmental process as it unfolds; a view, incidentally, that is impossible to obtain using conventional experimental methods. As Tina Bruce has remarked, Ben is an interesting blend of typical and atypical aspects of development. As in the first edition of the book, I will also use studies of 40 children, made over a two-year period, in a London nursery class, when I was a teacher. In this new edition I have added data from my recent research, conducted over a ten-year period, in Singapore. These studies are mostly of Chinese children but also include Malay and Indian children. I also include evidence from studies I made at Queensland University of Technology, of Australian children, in a nursery class in Brisbane, Australia. Additionally, I will also use studies of my two granddaughters – Joel's children, Keira and Poppy. In total, on my own, I have studied developmental sequences of over 100 children, though the majority of these are, of course, not as extensive and detailed as my first, longitudinal studies. Together with Sukitha Kunasegaran and Mariam Aljunied of the Psychological Assessment and Research Branch at the Ministry of Education, Singapore, I helped interpret 600 drawings made by Singaporean primary school children between ages six and twelve years. This resulted in a book about the evaluation (*not 'grading'*) of children's drawing, for all primary school teachers in Singapore (Kunasegaran, Aljunied and Matthews, 2002). The intention of all my work is to help teachers understand and appreciate children's development in drawing. My interpretation of the evidence from these studies combined, forms a quite different model of development from those of both traditional and some other recent theories.

Methodology

The studies of my own children were very detailed, based on day-to-day diaries of naturalistic observations. I did not test the children with a drawing task (unlike much recent work on children's drawing) but, rather, I chose to design naturalistic methods which captured what the children themselves were interested in and were trying to draw. This was also true of my studies of the 40 nursery children in the London nurseries in which I was a teacher. I continue to develop naturalistic methods throughout my studies of Singaporean children.

I started the studies using only physical notepad and pencil. There is a lot to be said for this method. Nowadays, I sometimes use three video cameras, each positioned at a different viewpoint. In this way I can capture three different sets of information about the same subject. This is particularly useful if I want to capture information about the interpersonal aspects of the process. For example, one camera will show the child's facial expressions and actions, another her drawing appearing on the paper, while the third might capture information of the whole context, including the caregiver's responses. (I got this idea from Colwyn Trevarthen's fascinating movies of mother and baby playing together.) I then edit together information from the three recordings and analyse the movies with the intention of constructing a description of development of representation within an interpersonal environment.

However, please note that, after many years of experience, I have developed very unobtrusive uses of video-recording with children. Sometimes the children themselves do the recording. The point I am stressing here is that insensitive research, no matter what kind of information technologies are used, will disrupt learning just as effectively as poor teaching.

I have developed my methodology of making observations of children's spontaneous behaviour, allowing children freedom to form their own representational structures. I do not try to distance myself from my subjects, either, but usually interact with them and talk to them. So my own interaction forms part of the data. I do not make experiments, in the true sense of the term, although in my more recent work I manipulate the contexts in various ways whenever it is necessary to tease out certain aspects which are difficult to capture in naturalistic studies. However, my approach remains essentially one of unobtrusiveness. Although I focus on drawing, and although I know that drawing is a special discipline with its own unique constraints and possibilities, I do not isolate drawing but observe it within its context of a family of emergent representational modes. To capture the real sense of representational development one needs the fullness of such descriptions; one has to see a representational act as a co-operation between a multiplicity of modes.

Although, when I started, my studies were criticised as being merely anecdotal and reliant on too small a sample (and a privileged one at that), recent writers have shown how necessary and important it is to learn about how a few individuals develop and learn (Thelen and Smith, 1994; Thelen et al. 2000). It is true that some information can only be gathered by experimental means and that one needs statistical pictures derived from large samples of children. However, as important as such studies are, the trouble is that they do not show *development*, but only highly generalised (and ultimately misleading) *stages* of development. Only longitudinal studies allow detailed understandings of the *process* of development. As Thelen and Smith so aptly put it, it is the *change* from one stage to another which is the most significant aspect, not the *stages* (so-called) themselves.

1

Painting in action

Ben, aged two, stands at a low table on which there is a sheet of paper and two pots of paint, one green and one blue. In each pot stands a paintbrush. First of all, Ben picks up the blue brush with his right hand and paints with it, using a vigorous fanning or arcing action from side to side across the surface of the paper. This action creates an elongated curved blue patch, like an arc of a large circle. His whole body seems involved in this energetic painting action.

The brush never leaves the surface of the paper but every now and then Ben abruptly changes his sideways fanning action to a pushing and pulling movement, to and from his chest. The paintbrush therefore moves in two opposing directions, from side to side, creating the blue arc, and this new, back and forth movement, crossing it at approximately 90 degrees, giving it a jagged contour.

Ben then puts this blue brush back in the pot and picks up the green brush. As he carries it over the painting, paint drips from it, leaving a trail of green spots across both the table and the painting. He notices this and immediately shakes the brush above the painting, making more green spots fall onto the white paper. In the meantime, Linda, his mother, has prepared a pot of red paint for him and has placed it, with a brush inside, on the table next to the other two pots. Picking this red brush he makes further arcing movements over the blue patch. The red mixes with the blue to make a brownish colour. He momentarily stops painting, and points with his left index finger to a particular part of the painting. The focus of his attention appears to be a section of the painted patch's irregular edge which his paintbrush has just produced. 'There's a car there', he says (see Figure 1).

Ben stops only for a moment, however, returning to his painting to make variations and combinations of the actions he has already produced. Arcing movements now flow into zigzag movements. The brush remains in contact

Figure 1   'There's a car there', by Ben, aged two

Figure 2   'It's going round the corner', by Ben, aged two

with the paper, even when, for a moment, he looks up at me and smiles.

Quickly turning back to his painting, Ben suddenly makes a quite different painting action. His brush describes a series of continuous, clockwise rotational movements. The first revolution runs right through the patch to which he had just referred as the 'car'. Each succeeding rotation almost coincides with the previous one. As he makes this continuous rotation he says, 'It's going round the corner ... It's going round the corner ... It's gone now' (see Figure 2). He then dips the brush into the red pot again and aims it into the roughly circular closed shape he has made. He repeatedly plonks the brush down with a quick, rhythmical stabbing motion. This makes red blobs

Figure 3   Ben, aged two, makes marks inside a closed shape

appear in and around the centre of the closed shape (see Figure 3).

Ben then vigorously smears these red blobs with the same brush, using that same horizontal arcing motion again. Very soon, the rotational shape and the small sector of white paper, which up to now remained within it, are obliterated under this energetic side-to-side movement of the brush.

Some questions

The above painting episode is typical of a kind practised by many two- to four-year-olds (Matthews, 1983; 1984; 1999). What does it mean? Is it a haphazard, random sequence of actions, without meaning? Is it mindless 'scribbling'? Many people would say that Ben is just messing around with paint. They might feel that this is neither an organised abstract design nor a drawing. Drawing, they might argue, is about making recognisable pictures or 'accurate' representations of objects, scenes and people. This child surely cannot be representing anything, since his painting is not a 'picture' of anything which we can recognise.

Even seeing Ben in the process of painting and hearing what he says about it would still fail to impress many people that anything significant was happening. They might agree that Ben enjoys this impulsive activity, but argue that it is just the clumsy beginnings of a long apprenticeship towards 'correct' drawing and painting. True, they might say, his actions seem intense, but surely much of his body movement is completely irrelevant to what drawing and painting are really about?

It is also true to say that he talks excitedly about the painting, but what is he talking about? Surely the only accurate term he uses is 'round' and we might expect young children to name a few shapes which accidentally occur in their paintings. How do we know that his words correspond to his painting? He mentions a 'car' but where is the 'car'? There does not appear to be a shape which accurately corresponds to a shape of a car. Surely his words are inappropriate and only have meaning for him?

This, after all, is the message given to us by the vast majority of books about the 'stages' of children's drawing development. Some writers on children's art acknowledge early mark-making as having emotional importance, or importance in terms of finding out about art materials, or in terms of the co-ordination of body movements and being able to use a paintbrush or pencil, but very few of them consider it to be the beginnings of visual representation or expression. Usually, it is called the 'scribbling' stage. One theory claims that scribbling is important only in so far as the child notices, and perhaps speaks about, accidental – or 'fortuitous' – likenesses appearing in the marks he or she has made. This theory continues with the child supposedly trying to purposely repeat what was initially the product of accident. This, in itself, is a startling idea, because, unlike what we know of any other aspect of intellectual development, the move to representation, from no representation at all is, according to this notion, simply a matter of accident. We will see later that accident does indeed play an important part of children's expression and representation, as it does in development overall, but not in the way it is described in the traditional theory.

A variation of this approach also starts with the notion that scribbling is important only in so far as it accidentally supplies a vocabulary of shapes out of which the child will, later on, make designs and pictures (Kellogg, 1969). According to this approach then, Ben's present painting actions, his actions in the here and now, are not in themselves important. They have significance only in terms of their supposed use later on in development. The explanation here would be that Ben stumbles upon the 'round' shape, recognises it as round (even uses the word 'round') and uses this and other shapes also discovered by happenstance as 'building blocks', put together to make designs and pictures of various kinds, perhaps months later. Although commonly accepted as an explanation, no one seems to have evidence that this process actually occurs (Cox, 1992; 1993; 1997). Ben uses the term 'round' as a verb, and as part of a sentence which describes an event. This is inexplicable in terms of either 'fortuitous realism' (accidental resemblances to things in the real world) or the theory that scribbling supplies a pool of geometric shapes for later compositions.

If people generally think the beginnings of drawing are disordered scribbling without meaning, then later drawings fare little better with many writers. Although children gradually learn to make pictures which adults think they recognise as attempts to represent views of objects, these images are at best regarded, in an uncritical, sentimental way, as charming or, worse still, thought to be full of errors. They are measured against a sort of checklist to see how well they conform to a notion of 'accurate representation'.

Sometimes, these attitudes are biased towards a restrictively Western European approach to representation originating from the Italian Renaissance in the fifteenth century. Although the terms 'visual realistic', 'accurate representation' and 'stages' trip off many a researcher's tongue, they are notoriously difficult to define and study.

The notion of 'visual realism' is not the only exemplar against which children's representation is measured. Other sorts of prejudices about representation are implicit in many accounts of children's drawing and influence the way people provide for the child to draw and paint. For instance, different societies might have different expectations of their children and these expectations will influence how children's visual representation is received. What these different exemplars have in common is that they define and measure development against a presumed end point in terms of a representational norm sanctioned as 'correct' by society.

At times, the ways in which we look at children's drawings and paintings conceals, rather than reveals, the meaning of painting episodes like Ben's. Jerome Bruner (1990) has commented that some kinds of research simply go round and round in circles, merely supporting the assumptions they are supposed to investigate. This happens when we emphasise how near to 'visual reality' children's drawings are, or compare them with some other notion of what makes for a 'good' or 'accurate' representation.

I believe that my research, over the last quarter of a century, in both London and Singapore, shows that children's drawing has organisation and meaning all the way from the beginning, when many people consider infants to be scribbling (see front cover illustration (top row, 2nd from left) and Figure 3a).

The way we understand and provide for children to draw and paint needs to be rethought. This does not just apply to art education. Children, as they begin to draw and paint, make an intellectual journey which has musical, linguistic, logical and mathematical as well as aesthetic aspects. All these are

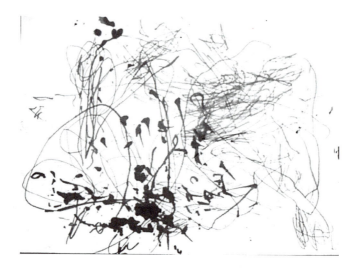

Figure 3a   A drawing by Ben, aged two years and three months

endangered if we do not understand the development of drawing. The familiar, positive clichés about children's art – that it contributes to cognitive development – are true. The problem has been that, as we shall see, with some notable exceptions (Smith, 1983; Wolf and Fucigna, 1983; Athey, 1990; Willats, 1997; Kindler, Eisner and Day, 2002 in press), few people have been able to say what this contribution actually is.

Visual representation and expression

Most people would accept that early mark-making is one aspect of a baby learning the skills of handling and using materials. We have to decide whether we are justified in claiming that this is also the beginning of visual representation and expression. Some writers suggest that, given what we know about other aspects of development, it would be strange if drawing had no meaning for the child, right from the start (Wolf and Fucigna, 1983; Athey, 1990). For example, recent research strongly suggests that right from birth, the baby develops a range of communicative and representational possibilities in actions and vocalisation. We know that newborn babies seem to be able to take part in shared acts of meaning with caregivers (Stern, 1977; Trevarthen, 1980; 1995). They also seem quickly to develop understandings about events and objects. Their mastery of objects seems to emerge from meaningful relationships with people, especially the first caregiver (Trevarthen, 1975; 1995). We shall return to this later.

Drawing and language

Language development is often seen as a continuous process which has meaning and organisation all the way through from its beginnings. Although there are many contrasting theories of how we learn to speak, many linguists would agree that the development of language is a creative process which cannot be explained as a process of imitation, by the infant, of adult speech. The work of Noam Chomsky (1966; 1994) shows that, even though young children's early speech might seem strange, it is the result of their active generation of language 'rules' which change as they grow older. We will see later the important analogy here to drawing development. Whether or not the notion of 'rule-making' is perfectly appropriate (for either language or drawing), and whether Chomsky's idea that these 'rules' are represented in the brain in some way, is controversial. Nevertheless, Chomsky's theory of the language acquisition as an essentially, *creative* process, in a technical sense, is very pertinent to drawing development. Children neither make sentences by copying older speakers, nor do they learn to draw by merely imitating adult pictures.

On the other hand, neither is development, in either language or drawing, completely idiosyncratic. Resolving the apparent contradiction between processes which seems to be at the same time both creative yet universal has been a perennial problem in describing development (Wilson and Wilson, 1985; Wilson, 1997). In any aspect of development, for example, learning to walk, children seem to move through similar sequences of development. We therefore expect children to start to walk around the first year, give or take a few months. Yet we each of us actually achieve our first steps in a unique way. The developmental route from crawling, or bouncing along on our bottoms, to cruising, to finally taking our first unsupported steps, is always individual and never predestined. How can these two aspects be simultaneously true? How can development in drawing, or in anything else, appear neat and orderly from a distance (to use Esther Thelen's and Linda Smith's apt way of putting it), yet messy and individualistic when viewed more closely (Thelen and Smith, 1994)? We clearly need better explanations than either the predictable 'stage-by-stage' theory, the imitation model or the notion that it is all totally individualistic. None of these are right.

Recent work in the origins of language also strengthens a link between language and other forms of representation. A long tradition in linguistics has been the notion that speech is a wholly arbitrary and conventional system of signs (unlike pictures, which resemble, in some way, the objects they represent). However, recent language studies offer evidence which suggests the origin of visual representation in a gestural language developed in infancy (Allott, 2001). This idea is very important for our later discussions about the beginnings and nature of visual expression and representation.

Scribbling and babbling

How then are we to understand what Ben is doing as he paints? When babies learn to speak, it might be the case that the rhythm, intonation and communicative patterns in babbling, along with the individual sounds, are carried over into the first true sentences (de Villiers and de Villiers, 1979; Allott, 2001; Thelen and Smith, 1994). I will argue that painting episodes like that of Ben, are grammatically articulated. He is obviously very involved in the painting at a level of communication and meaning. His whole manner suggests a commitment which would not be conveyed by mindless scribbling. What he is doing seems to be emotional. Perhaps it reflects or conveys his mood. Alternatively, it may help create a mood or, at least, intensify an existing one.

He seems to bring some understanding to the art materials he uses, and it is clear that he already knows a great deal about paint. He knows something about paint pots and brushes. He knows how to transport a paint-laden brush from the paint containers to the painting surface. He knows to reload the brush at intervals. Some kinds of knowledge, however, have been acquired in situations common to many children: investigating and playing with food and drink; studying the behaviour of water at bath-time. Ben knows a significant amount about contained liquids. It appears that drawing and painting actions are discovered from other actions previously explored. These earlier actions form a background upon which new actions are constructed. In turn, these new actions create further opportunities for more new actions, and so on. Drawing actions are members of a family of interacting expressive and representational actions formed against a history of earlier actions.

Ben has already learnt about the uses of the confines of the paper. For instance, he restricts most of his mark-making to this sheet. Arranging one's attention and actions towards a blank sheet of paper in readiness for the act of painting might be taken for granted by an adult. Yet even a blank sheet of paper is a product of a theory about space and representation developed over many years by a society. Before brush has been set to paper, Ben, in his attitude and stance, is doing something just as intelligent as using painting tools. This means that he has already acquired some insights into a particular mode of expression and representation. There is nothing extraordinary about Ben in this regard. Many children aged between two and three years will be introducing themselves to, or be introduced to, painting, writing and drawing media. It does suggest, however, that the way in which children discover, or are introduced to, these media, is important and affects their development.

Ben also has great command over a repertoire of actions which can be made with brush, paint and paper. These actions are organised and co-ordinated with his other knowledge of container and contained paint, so that he is able to respond to the behaviour of this liquid when it is set free by brushwork or spillage.

Horizontal arc

Babies learn to produce three basic mark-making movements which result in three basic marks (see Figures 4, 5 and 6). I think of these as First Generation marking actions. All the other marks and shapes will, during babyhood and early childhood, come out of these three marking actions. Ben's first mark-making gesture in this painting episode is one in which the brush is swung

Figure 4   Horizontal arc (at bottom of figure)

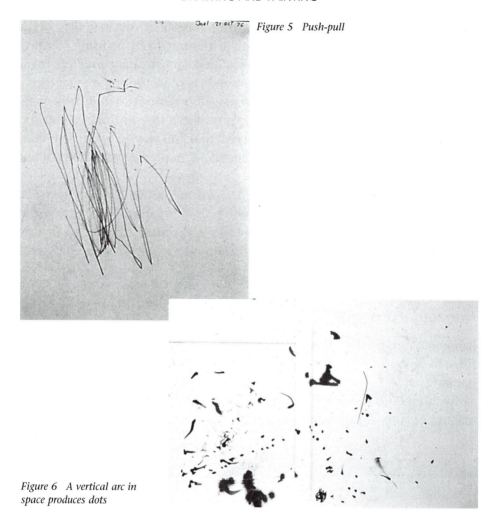

Figure 5   Push-pull

Figure 6   A vertical arc in space produces dots

or fanned from left to right, with the painting arm almost, but not quite, at fullest reach, with much of the movement coming from the shoulders and hips. This gesture describes an arcing shape; a patch of blue pigment which records a natural swing of the arm to and fro from the shoulder. It makes visible a normally invisible vector of body movement. As with all drawing actions, this mark-making gesture has emerged from actions made even earlier in infancy. I have called it the *horizontal arc* (Matthews, 1983; 1984; 1999) and its evolution will be described in the next chapter. It might be argued that this is surely a completely physical action, not necessarily indicative of intelligence. The observation records that, while painting, Ben even looked up at me for a moment. Is this not, then, the sort of painting action which could be made with one's eyes closed? No. Research shows that this explanation is not justified.

It is not just the movement which is important to children in their early drawings. In experiments, children quickly abandoned 'dummy' pens which failed to leave a mark (Gibson and Yonas, 1968; Berefelt, 1987). When young children paint or draw, they do occasionally look elsewhere and rely momentarily on information from special sensors in their joints (proprioceptive information) which tells them about the positions of their limbs. However, careful observation shows that they quickly return and look at the drawing, not only to make sure the marking tool is merely 'on course', as in driving a car, but also to engage more deeply in this expressive event, and sometimes (as in Ben's case) to engage the attention of another person. Sometimes, having regained visual contact, children produce a little burst of speed (Matthews, 1992).

The very notion that drawing might be 'merely' physical is, to this writer, wrong-headed anyway. Painting, like any other activity, is multimodal, involving kinaesthetic, proprioceptive, haptic as well as visual information. The traditional division between what is considered sensorimotor and the mental activity is an artificial and meaningless one.

The importance of other people

Young children look away from their activities to check on their surroundings and on any recent occurrence. They also look away from what they are doing to look at those very special objects, people. They do this to check their whereabouts and to gauge, engage or maintain the level of interest of these onlookers. Sometimes, the pace and organisation of the painting is influenced by subtle responses from the adult. When, for example, Ben looks back from me to the painting, his sudden production of a very different drawing action – an elliptical motion of the brush – might be a response to my interest. This is a part of the social and interpersonal context in which children make meaning as they draw. The development of children's drawing and painting (or any intellectual or physical skill) does not come about completely by itself. The attitude of the people around the child has a profound effect. The general direction of the child's developmental journey, at least in infancy and early childhood, and each twist and turn from moment to moment, is influenced by the responses of surrounding people and by society at large. This is a crucially important point and one over which there is much confusion. There are two major mistakes: (1), no support at all, and (2), just as bad, damaging adult interference and domination.

In some respects, painting for the very young is like a conversation and has a conversational structure to it. Detailed analysis of the actions involved in early painting would seem to confirm this. Many early painting and drawing episodes are composed of rapidly alternating bursts of action, each unit of action suggestive of a particular idea, similar to the short bursts of words (termed 'intonational units' by Chafe, 1994, p. 57), which embody ideas in a conversation. Again, like speech, these passages or bursts of action in such painting and drawing sequences are related to the infant's breathing patterns (Matthews, 2000a). Later, we will see other relationships between the structure of language and that of early painting and drawing.

First, this conversation may involve an adult, but later on the child might be able to maintain the conversation on his or her own. Early adult support of children's activities makes possible the development of this conversation, so that, eventually, young children achieve autonomy and can engage in a conversation solely with the art materials themselves. To a great extent, this is already happening with Ben, but this is made possible by the subtle support he has from his parents, Linda and me. We will return to the importance of adult help for young children later on.

An opposing, and I believe, mistaken belief about children's visual representation, is that development in the child's use of visual media happens completely naturally without any kind of assistance. In fact, some pioneers of child art (for example, Franz Cizek, Rhoda Kellogg and Frances Derham) sometimes give the impression that adult influence is actually damaging to children's creativity and is to be avoided (White and Stevenson 1997). It is certainly true that some kinds of adult influence damage children's developing in representation and expression (Bruce, 1991). Sometimes the thinker has to be a loner. At present, with the focus of criticism on 'laissez-faire' approaches, this is a subtle but crucial point which is in danger of being forgotten. However, support of a subtle and special kind is needed from adults if we want children's drawing, painting and construction to really flourish (Athey, 1990; Eisner, 1997; Kindler, 1997a; 1997b; Matthews, 1984; 1994; 1999; 2002 in press).

Another misconception about children's development and learning is that children neither initiate any learning by themselves nor play any significant role in the learning process. According to this view, children are basically empty vessels and the task of education is to 'fill' them with knowledge. Sometimes this idea is blurred with another, which was mentioned above, that learning comes about by children simply copying adult exemplars.

When curriculum designers have these ideas it can be very destructive to children's learning, especially when education is planned only in terms of sets of knowledge and skills to be transmitted to children. This undermines children's internally driven and dynamic process of learning. The so-called education 'reforms', inflicted on schools for the last twenty years or so in the UK and elsewhere, are not guided by knowledge of development but in terms of programmes of instruction based upon assumptions about what constitutes the discipline or subject (Kelly, 1990). Though thinly disguised in dubious developmental 'stages', the English National Curriculum in Art falls into this category (Matthews, 2001b; Atkinson, 2002 forthcoming).

We will return to the ideas of the social context for development throughout the book, but suffice it to say at this point that we, indeed, are looking at a naturally unfolding sequence of development. It has become fashionable to 'knock' the pioneers of children's art for perhaps underestimating the role of society, but they did get something right. They did understand that some forms of so-called 'teaching' are destructive to development. They were reacting to the Victorian aftermath of extremely repressive and regimented 'still-life' and copying lessons (Matthews, 2001a; 2001b; Piscitelli, 2001; Matthews, 2002 in press). They did understand that there was something universal about children's art, something vital and creative, as many of the pioneers of modern art realised too.

However, some enthusiasts of children's art may have underestimated the special role people have to play in providing the kinds of experiences which encourage and promote this development. As Athey (1990) has described, development is to do with an interaction between what is unfolding within the child and what is available within the environment. Although 'interaction', 'scaffolding' and 'intervention' have become fashionable terms, these are sometimes interpreted extremely badly or used as a blanket to hide holes in our understanding. It is always perilous to have covered holes around.

Precisely what form then, should this interaction take? We have decided that some forms of interaction are destructive, and we know that children do not borrow just everything and anything from the environment. So, what, then, is the mechanism of this interaction?

Chance plays a part in it, because it causes a multiplicity of different kinds of encounter with objects and situations. However, development is far from being a completely random process. It is like an evolutionary process (Darwin, 1859). The child randomises explorative and investigative actions in such a way as to generate a fertile ground of representational possibilities. The child is constantly, actively, purposely, seeking out those particular experiences which will promote growth. This happens in different ways and at different levels; at a large-scale or 'macro' level, in which the child makes choices about which objects to investigate and which events to participate in; and at small-scale or 'micro' levels, in which rapid decisions are made about actions performed upon materials. We can see this micro-level in the way Ben varies the tempo and direction of his painting actions. Video recordings show that when young children use paint, their movements are far from merely mechanical in the muscles and joints; they look at what they do, and can vary what they do intentionally. They show and use knowledge; knowledge about the body and its potential in terms of action within specific contexts. Early childhood painting is a stunning example of a process of fluid adaptation to unique circumstances which co-ordinates and combines object mastery with the exploitation of body actions for expressive or representational messages.

Painting actions – varying the tempo and direction

Ben varies his arcing movement by flexing his elbow and he shortens the length of this arc occasionally, to fill in blank areas he has noticed. When he sees such an area, his posture changes; he hunches over the painting, intently concentrating on these new targets. He also relocates the starting point of the arc, re-targeting the brush at this position. None of this behaviour seems merely mechanical. On the contrary, the variations he makes suggest rapid and complex decision-making. He selects areas for painting. In other words, he already knows something about two-dimensional area and the brushwork needed to fill it.

Push-pull

His horizontal arcing, to and fro, of the brush is occasionally altered to a push-pulling action, creating an oscillating, zigzagging line. The beginnings of this push-pull gesture (Matthews, 1983; 1984; 1999) will be studied in the next chapter. One effect of the push-pull is to disrupt the boundary of the curved shape. It becomes a jagged, irregular contour. It produces ragged boundaries of paintwork in which shapes are created. Children notice these shapes and are attracted to them. Ben's push-pull action produces a small patch of colour which sticks out from the boundary of the blue arc. This shape might not seem important, yet, for Ben, it is. After he has made this little shape, he stops painting, looks at it and suddenly points at it with his left index finger, saying, 'There's a car there'.

Dynamic patterns of action

The child brings to these materials actions she has discovered and developed in a number of contexts. Jean Piaget (1951) described such repeatable actions as *schemas*, which the child uses in many different situations (Athey, 1990, p. 35). When the same, or similar action is applied in different contexts and upon different objects, the child receives valuable information about the object and how the movement has affected the object. Ben uses a grasping schema on long objects such as spoons. Piaget would have said that he adapts this grasping schema when holding another, new, long object, a brush. Piaget thought of these action schemas as gradually being internalised or interiorised to form patterns of thought. He thought that some kinds of schemas formed blueprints for actions, like holding a brush (a *dynamic action* schema) and that others became mental images of things (a *figurative* schema), for example, a mental picture of a brush. More recently, other writers have thought of these actions as *attractors*, not stored as representations in the brain, as Piaget thought, but emerging in specific contexts. Thelen and Smith (1994) describe two sorts of 'attractor systems', each focused on a different aspect of objects and events, which they term the 'what' and 'where' aspects. Work in neuroscience also confirms two streams of visual information in the human visual system, one that carries 'where' information and one that carries 'what' information (Eliot, 1999). These correspond approximately to the configurative (shape) and the dynamic aspects (movement) of objects and events. 'What' and 'where' attractors flow into each other to make more complex sequences of action and also to form dynamic categories which can be both more generalised or differentiated when set in motion by similar or related stimuli. For example, Ben combines his horizontal arcing gesture with his push-pulling gesture. This combination produces a new shape, a patch of colour which he says is a 'car'.

Representing shape and movement

What does Ben mean by this? He seems to be using the shape of the patch to stand for the shape of the car. The representation suggests the shape of an object. It is a *figurative representation*. A moment later, he makes a very different kind of movement – the *continuous rotation* of the brush (Athey, 1990; Matthews, 1983; 1984; 1999). This is a very important drawing action for the child and we will see how it develops later in the book. With this different action, Ben also makes a different kind of representation, an *action representation*.

Ben uses the rotational, round and round movement of the brush to represent, not the car's shape, but its movement in time and space. While the brush is in motion, Ben says, 'It's going round the corner … It's going round the corner'. He uses the brush's 'trace-making effects' (Michotte, 1963, p. 289) to show the passage of movement of the car. He also uses other kinds of changes going on in the paint. For example, when the paint line loses contrast against the blue patch and disappears, he says, 'It's gone now'.

The comings and goings of objects, the different ways they come in and out of sight, are very important to the young child. We will see this idea influencing painting and drawing in different ways and at different levels during babyhood and childhood. With the exception of Wolf and Fucigna (1983) and Athey (1990), this type of representation seems to have gone unnoticed by the majority of researchers. Although, more recently, there has been some acknowledgement of this mode of representation, its significance is yet to be fully grasped by the majority of psychologists of drawing, those in art education and those in early years education. There is a tendency to think of representation as a *re*-presentation of a prior experience. Associated with this idea, there is still a strong tendency to think of '*re*-presentation' as synonymous with 'picturing'. But, although representation does often try to make sense of previous experience, it is not a copy of that experience. Representation is an essentially dynamic, constructive act which shapes the experience itself.

Because of a long history of what one might call the misrepresentation of representation, an ingrained habit of thinking has grown that 'good' pictures faithfully reflect an absolute reality, somewhere 'out there', beyond the picture surface. Consequently, a painting activity like Ben's, in the observation above, is not considered representational at all. Action representation has rarely been described and its relationship to the development of drawing is yet to be fully understood. My recent studies suggest that this intense participation with painting actions may have a strong influence on later representation.

There are many questions to be asked about action representations. In Ben's painting, for example, where precisely is the representation taking place? Is it in the paint-trails, the brush's movements or in his moving arm? Equally, it is difficult to say exactly what the lines and shapes stand for. On the other hand, perhaps this is not the best way to approach an understanding of this form of representation. Perhaps it is closer to the truth to describe this as a 'collaboration' (using the term in the way that artist Robert Rauschenberg perhaps intended [Brown, 1997, p. 268]), with an unfolding representational event which combines together a family of co-ordinated sensory and communicative channels. Perhaps it is meaningless to try to divide it up into aspects which happen to fit adult categorisations of subject-areas or disciplines. It is the very repleteness of such episodes which conveys and captures the child's profound emotional and intellectual engagement with the representation of events and objects (Wolf, 1984). We will see later, how such emergent 'ideas' about representations are 'transported' (to use Dennie Wolf's [Wolf and Fucigna, 1983, p.1] term) across a variety of symbolic and representational domains.

Some of Ben's ideas are to do with *shape*, *location* and *movement*. We should not be too surprised that these concerns are reflected in this very early painting. They were there from birth, when he learnt to visually track moving objects. These concerns are also reflected in language, which seems to be divided into *dynamic* or *stative* aspects, that is, language is divided into utterances about either the states of things or the states of events. As noted above, neuroscience suggests that the human perceptual system is divided into two kinds, one devoted to finding out where things are, while another finds out about what things are. Some have thought this must be due to innate conceptions of events and objects (Spelke, 1985; 1990); others have proposed that dynamic systems of interaction between the baby's perceptual system and the environment are set in motion by certain stimuli (Thelen and Smith, 1994; Thelen et al., 2000). Whichever way this might be represented internally, in the central nervous system, it is represented externally in painting, drawing and three-dimensional activities, plus dance-like and musical actions. This discussion will be followed up in the next chapter. One of children's tasks in early representations is to co-ordinate understandings of shape, location and movement together. It may be no accident that Ben's first revolution of the brush runs perfectly through the centre of the patch which represents the 'car'. He may be interested in the idea that the same object which was stationary and which occupied a single position in space, can move.

Understandings formed in representational play with small, handheld toys are carried over from medium or activity to another. For example, Ben may be pushing the paintbrush to emulate pushing a stationary object into motion, rather like the way he pushes his toy cars into motion. By allowing transfer of ideas across the boundaries of different domains or processes or media, there occurs a mutually reciprocal feedback in which the child makes essentially the same action but sees different effects as the actions impact upon different media. This process is a conversation with materials and media. The teaching implications are important. Educational plans which stress the supposed divisions and boundaries between subject areas discourage this cross-association of ideas, so essential if the child is to co-ordinate different kinds of knowledge into an entire description of reality. It will also discourage true creative and innovative thinking precisely because it focuses the learner's attention on the divisions between different kinds of knowledge, rather than the connections. We will see in later chapters how drawing and painting are perfectly suited for a child to investigate what, how and why things move or do not move, and what happens to them when they disappear.

Closed shape

The rotational movement of the brushstrokes forms a roughly circular *closed shape*. Ben loads a brush with red paint and stabs it at approximate right angles to the paper's surface within the boundaries of the closed shape. This results in blobs enclosed within the closed shape. The closed shape is an important visual structure in drawing development. With this form, Ben, like most other children, will use it to represent the spatial relationship *inside and outside*.

The discovery and use of the closed shape will be described more fully in Chapter 4.

Painting as a patterned dance in space and time

Ben's painting is like that of many young children. It is a rhythmical, patterned dance or play with paint and body actions in space and time. There are different starting points, a network of intricately timed entrances and exits, interpenetrating plots and sub-plots, and a variety of stopping points.

When Ben finally obliterates the close shape and its red nuclei under a vigorous arcing of the brush, this is one of many 'curtain-closing' acts. The multimodal nature of Ben's painting actions means that it is not helpful to cut up the episode into fragments. It is precisely the interrelationships between sensory-perceptual modes which give it its richly layered meaning.

Play

Play makes all this possible. Play is implicated in the development of all forms of representation (Bruce, 1991). Although pushed to the periphery of contemporary education, the intellectual and emotional depths of play are profound. During the period when his painting was produced, Ben moved a handheld toy car around the home, often talking softly to himself as he went. He often referred to the direction of the car, also ideas about the starting point of the car and its destination or point of arrival. This idea formed an important part of his painting scenario. When he refers to a 'car ... going round the corner' while painting, he has 'transported' (to use Dennie Wolf's, [1983, p. 1] term) a familiar scenario from his play with toy cars over into the activity of painting. Now, a handheld brush replaces the handheld toy car, as if the brush has become the toy. What is the significance of this?

Play is difficult to define but indispensable to learning. When children struggle to master actions, objects and skills, or when they try to understand something new, as when Ben learned to grasp a brush, put it in a pot and lift out the paint without spilling it, children adapt their actions and their thinking to the demands of these specific tasks and objects. Piaget called this process *accommodation*. This is not play. In this situation children are struggling to attain action and object-mastery.

Play allows us a completely different attitude. When children play, they temporarily free their actions from the restrictions imposed upon them by the demands of the situation. They can change the situation to fit their own behaviour. Piaget called this process *assimilation*. The distinction between playful and non-playful actions is a useful one, but in real situations, accommodation and assimilation might flow into each other. Investigation, exploration, object-mastery and representation may follow each other in rapid-fire succession.

The concept of play is implicated in the child's understandings and use of symbols, signs and representations. Children need opportunities to temporally uncouple means from ends in tasks, allowing them the opportunity to investigate processes as entities of interest in themselves and worthy of repetition. In Vygotskian terms, play allows the child to separate words from objects, and actions from meanings (Vygotsky, 1966). This has some important consequences for learning. By releasing objects and actions from their usual

functions and meanings, the child is able to detect characteristics not otherwise revealed when these objects, and the actions performed upon them, are
tied to adaptation to object-mastery. It might sound paradoxical, but it is by
liberating actions and objects from their usual functions that the child is able
to construct an objectifiable universe (Lorenz, 1996). When objects and action
are set free from their constraints in adaptation to reality, this allows the child
to form the combinatorial flexibility noted by Bruner (1964) so necessary if a
deep reading and use of semiotic systems is to occur. This ludic process allows
hybrid families of thoughts and ideas to be formed within hypothetical or analogue realities in which they can be tested. Play provides a safe psychological
space for children to think about frightening realities. In play, children can run
and rerun the disappearance and reappearance of significant objects and
people, so as to get used to their feelings about how things, and people, come
and go, where they are when they are 'gone' and how they might return
(Freud, 1915–17; Easthope, 1999). Ben's staging of the 'car', 'going around the
corner' and 'gone now', is such an instance.

Splattering paint

Ben lifts the loaded brush and droplets of paint splatter from it. At this point,
he does not appear to consider this an 'accident'. He does not attempt to 'correct' the action. On the contrary, he extends it on purpose, by shaking the
brush to cause more drops to splatter onto the paper. He is using the skills
and understandings he has already developed, about inertial forces, which
enables him to splatter droplets from the shaken brush.

The accidental release of droplets of paint might trigger off, in his brain,
what has been called an *attractor system* (Thelen and Smith, 1994; Thelen et al.,
2000) which then calls up a related attractor, related 'knowledge' derived from
prior experiences of shaking a wet or messy object so that droplets fly off.

However, these techniques are not used with a fixed end in mind, but are
of interest in themselves as the currency of free-play. This is also true of the
unpredictable events these techniques set in train. This does not mean that
just about anything could happen. The sequence of events Ben follows is
guided by attractor systems or patterns of action already set up in his brain
and ready to go.

It is a dynamic, chaotic situation in which many different, structural and
representational possibilities 'surface', literally and metaphorically speaking.
Self-motion is particularly important because it allows a multiplicity of 'takes'

to be made of the same situation, building a complex, 'dynamic assembly' of understandings which eventually can be reconfigured in many ways (Thelen and Smith, 1994, p. 194).

Ben is completely involved in what he is doing with the paint on the paper. Whatever happens he will incorporate it into the painting. When he lifts a brush, moves it to the surface, or trails it on the surface, different things happen. He has to make quick-fire decisions from moment to moment. His choice of one course of action rather than another is influenced by his past history of interactions, and the intrinsic dynamics of the present situation. Development may set off through any one of a number of new potential developmental directions, when an action falls, as it were, into a nearby dynamic attractor in this developmental landscape through which he is moving. Although Piaget thought of these as internal schemas like plans or blueprints for action it is more probable that we are seeing a dynamic system unfold, which, although based upon a matrix genetically formed through evolution, is not, in itself preformed in the brain, but rather a process in which the child takes advantage of the avenues of action which present themselves to him from moment to moment. What causes him to take one course of action rather than another is not due to internal plans or blueprints for action, as Piaget thought, but rather 'biases' or 'values' (Edelman, 1987; Thelen and Smith, 1994; Thelen et al., 2000) caused by the potential developmental pathways and the potential direction in which they head. Gradually, complex overlappings of different attractor systems will cause generalisable, dynamic categories, the 'primitives' of thought (Thelen and Smith, 1994; Thelen et al., 2000).

There are two types of basic attractor systems set off with emergent representation. One traces around the contours of shapes in terms of action, while another system records the features of objects. Gradually, the child learns the names for shapes ('round', for example) and this word may cause families of attractors to form around it. The word acts like a 'pivot' around which utterances, and linguistic, visual and kinaesthetic representations (to do with movement and the sensation of movement), are formed.

Ben's act of painting is a dynamic balance between what he wants to do and how it turns out. Although some of what he does is accidental, he makes use of accident and incorporates it into a continuous conversation between what he wants to do and what in fact happens. The accidental has been overemphasised in studies of how children draw and paint. Children's early painting is not so much random as purposefully *randomised*, in order that a wealth of possibilities and meanings may be harvested. If you think about it, it is not straightforward to define what is meant by the word 'control'. Skilled artists, performers and sportspeople do not rigidly control their actions. Take a footballer for example. She will allow a certain amount of fluidity and flexibility into her performance in order that she can immediately respond to whatever unknown future event unfolds in the game.

The idea of the accident versus the intended or 'correct' derives again from classical models of development. One influential account of children's drawing, which still affects people's thinking, comes from the work of two men, Piaget (1951) and Luquet (Luquet, 1927; Costall, 2001). Luquet was a great pioneer of children's drawing and had some extraordinarily sensitive insights about it (Luquet, 1927; 2001). Luquet noticed many of the most significant aspects of children's drawing and asked many of the questions still raised today. He had a great understanding about how children's art might best be supported by adults. Luquet discovered that children alternate between different *modes* of representation – an idea of profound significance. Piaget used Luquet's ideas in his own theory of cognitive development. However, he arranged these modes of representation into a 'staged' hierarchy, with children climbing from the supposedly lowest (most inferior) at the bottom (or at the beginning of development) in successive steps towards the highest (most superior), at the top (or end of development). This was not what Luquet intended at all. Luquet considered all the modes that children used to be equally valid. He stressed the 'realism' of each mode – not just the 'realism' of the visually realistic model (Costall, 1993; 1995; 2001). In contrast, Piaget's model describes children's development in visual representation as a progression through distinct stages starting with 'scribbling' and, with successive 'corrections', culminating in a correct, 'visually realistic' picture. Because it is still very influential, we should look a little more closely at this theory.

The first stage in this hierarchy is usually thought to be meaningless 'scribbling'. From here, the story goes, children stumble upon accidental or 'fortuitous' likenesses appearing in their drawings, which they then try to purposely repeat. In fact, there is scant evidence to support this traditional notion (Cox, 1992; 1993).

This classic theory continues with stages of, first, 'intellectual realism' and then 'visual realism'. During 'intellectual realism', children produce drawings which most adults recognise as representations of objects but nevertheless still find strange, because such drawings do not show a realistic *view* of an object. These drawings are often termed *intellectually realistic*, the idea being that they capture what the child intellectually understands about the object (or scene), rather than the optical shape of the object projected to the eye held still at a fixed position. Boiled down to its simplest form, intellectually realistic drawings are supposed to show what the child *knows* rather than what the child *sees*. The stage of intellectual realism is supposed finally to be replaced by the next stage, in which the situation is reversed, and the child now draws what he or she *sees*, rather than what he or she *knows*. The drawings produced in this stage are often termed *visually realistic*.

This is a strange theory of development for a number of reasons. For one thing, although some children's drawings might be approximately categorised like this. Some of the drawings which illustrate this book (see Figures 42, 43 and 45) arguably contain 'intellectually realistic' information. However, in other ways they fit only uncomfortably into these groups (Costall, 1995; Matthews, 2001a). More fundamentally, it is meaningless to attempt to separate 'seeing' from 'understanding.' As will be later discussed, when we look at things, it is not a photographic process but one which involves logic, language, feelings and one which is driven by predispositions and desires.

There are aspects of very young children's drawing which seem to fit into the Piaget/Luquet model of development. For instance, when Ben makes a patch which he then names a 'car', surely this sounds like a case of 'fortuitous realism'? In fact, although it does appear that, by chance, the child sometimes stumbles upon a resemblance in her marking, this ignores the fact that she is exploiting an entire range of possibilities of which the occasional accidental likeness is but one. Ben, like other children, purposely set up situations in which accident (for want of a better word) is likely to happen. While it is true that at the beginnings of painting and drawing, children are not always in control of skidding brushes and splattering paint, the idea that accident is the main mechanism of development is simply not true – a fact that Luquet himself noted in his book in 1927. He realised that drawing was a complex activity which combined many strategies. Early drawing is like a dialogue between what the child wants to do and what appears on the paper. The child takes advantage of different kinds of opportunities which arise out of this interaction. The child notices, not only shapes of things but the shapes of events too. To wonder whether or not these events, set in motion by the brush, are accidental, is perhaps to miss the point. In a continuous conversation with the unfolding event of the painting process, the child seizes opportunities in many different modes and at many different levels. The child is not so much making random actions as purposely randomising action, in order that a wealth of possibilities emerge.

By supporting children's paintings and drawing we are empowering them, because by helping them form hypothetical and analogue realities in their representation we are giving them some way of controlling their lives. Ben is not only gaining motor-control and mastery of painting materials, but is developing ideas too. To separate these two aspects, sensorimotor actions and thought, is symptomatic of a major misunderstanding about emotional and intellectual development which has had destructive consequences for teaching. Ben represented and explored his feelings about the possession of power. He created a car on the paper, using paint. It is important to appreciate that the 'car going round the corner' would have a driver who could possibly be Ben. He may be thinking about his control of the power, speed and noise of the engine. Ben may be using this representational act, as other children would, to play with the feeling of mastery. He is therefore not only gaining power over the painting tools themselves but also over the visual changes and events taking place in the behaviour of paint, which simultaneously refer to hypothetical realities beyond the painting surface. We could think of this as the *structure* of the painting. The representation of driving the car may, at a deeper level, represent his own desire to be in control of power, movement and the outcome of events. Being able to control disappearance and reappearance of a significant object or person is an illusion but an essential one for the human infant (Freud, 1915–17; Easthope, 1999). We could think of this level as the *content* of the painting. It is important to note that the term 'content', as used here, does not only refer to the surface 'pictorial' content of the painting (the subject matter – 'car – going around the corner') but the deeper content of the identity and destiny of objects. It is important to remember the difference between the structure and content of the child's painting and drawing and how these interlock.

As I mentioned earlier, verbal language may derive from actions of the body. The concept of 'going around' is a good example; when this is made in speech, children and adults sometimes mime with a circular movement of the finger and arm, a circular movement in space and time. It may be that both single words and utterances are composed of units of articulation of the body. Ben's painting may be a visual 'utterance' (Allott, 2001; Matthews, 1999; 2000a).

Drawing and language

The above approaches to representation and expression are little understood and have received scant attention. The way children represent in their drawings and paintings has been concealed rather than revealed through the definitions used. Carolee Fucigna (1983, p. 1) points out that there was a similar problem in early studies of language development. This has had a bad effect on education and childcare. Language development moves along a continuum which has organisation and meaning right from the first sounds. This is true of all aspects of representation, of which language is but one. Recently, in contrast with the theory that language is an arbitrary set of conventional sounds, some theorists claim that language, like drawings, has its roots in physical action and gesture. This would suggest that all forms of representation originate from the same source and are unified within an interacting system, rather than a set of distinctly different ways of thinking, as has been suggested by Howard Gardner (1985; 1997). We will return to this important idea later.

Piaget thought that, in the beginning of language acquisition, children used words in a personal and idiosyncratic way. According to Piaget, the child initially thought that the name of the object – the word for it – was a part of the object. As Allott (2001) notes, although nowadays Piaget's ideas about language receive severe criticisms, the idea that the child initially thinks of the object and the word as one and the same is an important insight. Words and objects are deeply connected in representational systems in the brain. It is through play that the child learns to separate words from objects and actions from meanings (Vygotsky, 1966).

As babies learn to speak, they often practise sounds over and over again to themselves. At such times, they are not calling anyone but playing with the possible combinations and variations of sounds. It is essential for language development that they do this. They learn about the structure of speech which they could not achieve by simply copying from older speakers. They are well motivated to do this. They find speech sounds and speech actions interesting in themselves. Derek Bickerton (1981, p. 234) calls this 'infrastructural motivation'. It means that babies are motivated to find out how sounds are put together to make meaning.

The same is true of drawing. Children investigate and play with patterned sequences of actions, and repeat, vary and combine these according to how they look and feel in terms of shapes, colours, lines and movements. There is more to this than the child just assembling a formal vocabulary of shapes, in the way that Rhoda Kellogg (1969) thought. On the one hand, the child realises that drawing is made out of self-sufficient shapes and, unlike many adults, the child never suffers from the delusion that drawings and paintings are imitations of the visible world (Rawson, 1982; Golomb, 1974; 1992;

1993). On the other hand, the child also sees that there is a relationship between these visual structures and structures in the real world. It is this 'double-knowledge' (Furth, 1969) or dual nature of visual representation, that a shape on a piece of paper can 'stand for' something quite other than itself, which makes representation possible (Stetsenko, 1995). Anna Stetsenko has argued that drawing may be the perfect medium to show up this dual nature of symbols, signs and representations.

The child carries the understandings she forms across media domains. Opportunities and support for this transference are crucial for the growth of creative and independent thinking.

Summary

In this chapter, we have seen that very young children form some powerful approaches to representation and expression during the time when they are supposed to be merely scribbling. It turns out that, in contrast to traditional theory and popular conventional wisdom, children rarely scribble. The start of visual representation in early childhood has been badly misunderstood by researchers, if recognised at all. This is largely because of researchers' preconceptions or assumptions about what a painting or drawing is. For example, Steven Pinker, arguing for the theory of neurological modularity of the brain and against the idea of the brain as a sort of all-purpose, symbol-making device, writes of the 'grammatical genius' of very young children while simultaneously claiming that 'a three year old … is quite incompetent at the visual arts' (Pinker, 1994, p. 19). Yet, before they can barely talk, infants are already forming a visual language of great eloquence and meaning. We should not be too surprised by this, given what we know about other aspects of the beginnings of representational thought. Language may have its roots in this gestural and visual language of infancy. This is a very different idea from the one that claims distinct and separate channels of different 'intelligences' (Gardner, 1985; 1997; Pinker, 1994).

The infant has the need to investigate profound realities of shape, location and movement. Where am I? What is happening? These are perhaps the first questions we pose ourselves when surprisingly finding ourselves on a new planet. What things are, where things are, where things go, where did I last leave them, whether they will ever come back, are basic concerns which last until the end of life.

One approach to children's art is an uncritical sentimentality that children's drawings and paintings are delightful outpourings which will be damaged by any form of adult influence or teaching. This idea has been rightly criticised by many. However, there is an equally disastrous, contrasting approach which receives little criticism nowadays. Indeed, it gets wholehearted support from governments. Many researchers assume that the end point of drawing development is when children make pictures of how three-dimensional objects appear as if seen from a fixed position in space. Following their advice, teachers are encouraged to stamp out the spontaneous drawing of childhood and correct children until they make 'good' representations. This other extreme is just as bad as the romantic, laissez-faire approach. Many teachers would vehemently deny that the goal of their teaching is visual realism and it is true that, nowadays, between the laissez-faire position and the deficit model, there are many shades and variants of the presumed goal of children's representation. However, what these different desired end states all have in common is the idea that children's development is best described in terms of supposed deficits in need of correction until the form of representation socially sanctioned by society (whether this be pre-modern, modern, or postmodern makes little difference) is reached.

How one conceptualises what is going on in children's drawing and how children develop will have very a profound influence on the ways one goes about planning educational experiences for the very young. This in turn will have repercussions for older childhood and adolescence, too. If you feel that development in drawing is a wholly natural development, which is basically unteachable, then this will lead to a laissez-faire approach. If, on the other hand, you feel that children's drawings are deviant and incorrect versions of a more superior form of representation to come, then you will consider that children are in need of correction until the 'desired outcome' is attained. Even at the beginning of the twenty-first century, this is often couched in terms of a training in techniques to show depth, viewpoint and three-dimensional volumes as if seen from a notional viewing position.

All these approaches are anachronistic when we consider the range of practices considered as drawings by contemporary artists (for example, see Rose, 1992; Button and Esche, 2000; Pietronigro, 2000). But, more importantly, such approaches are very damaging to development. It becomes ever more urgent to identify these neglected ways of expression and representation and to help young children develop them. If we do not, we have no basis for planning for learning. Without good theory, education, and the terms in which it is defined, will continue to be hijacked and corrupted by a vacuous consumerist paradigm which (with a few notable exceptions) dominates education today.

Drawing is a continuum which is organised and meaningful right from the outset

Children start to represent both the shape of objects and their movement. They start to use the event of painting to represent other events beyond the surface of the painting. These may be hypothetical events in hypothetical worlds, or they may be a record of thinking and feeling more difficult to pin down in words. In a process similar in certain respects to language development, children investigate the pattern or structure of their drawing and the actions which make them. They also imbue painting actions with a range of emotions. Even in the hands of a two-year-old, painting and drawing become sensitive media, responsive to delicate fluctuations in mood.

What is the best way to support and encourage development?

How do we support this process? A knowledge of, and interest in, art is extremely useful but, on its own, is insufficient. Also needed is a knowledge of children's development in visual representation. This has to be understood properly before any teaching and learning experiences can be planned. This is one of the reasons why the English Art Curriculum is so poor. It is defined in terms of a definition of 'art' and its so-called 'basic elements' and how to teach these to children (Matthews, 2001b).

Yet, however much government hacks tinker around with the curriculum, to make it sound more up-to-date, such definitions can only be provisional and are not central to education. What is more important is that caregivers and teachers learn what are the experiences within the supposed discipline or subject area (be it 'art' or anything else), in terms of experiences and processes, which actually promote development.

Moreover, it is very important to reassess children's spontaneous art and unsupervised activities. These are undervalued, if not actively repressed, in contemporary school curricula for reasons of social control. The child creates art from a background of other actions already discovered and exercised. Out of the seemingly chaotic actions of the infant, there is articulated a gestural language on which symbolisation will be built. Without this language in place, no further learning is possible.

2

Actions, skills and meaning

Where do representations of movement and objects come from?

Early mark-making is a member of a family of interrelated expressive and representational actions. In the previous chapter, the observation of Ben painting showed that he was representing the movement, shape and location of an object. Where did these understandings and abilities come from?

Recent studies of newborn babies suggest that expressive thought begins at, or soon after, birth (Spelke, 1985; Trevarthen, 1995; Thelen and Smith, 1994; Thelen et al., 2000). This is very different from the idea of the baby as a blank slate. Studies reveal that when babies enter the world they are quickly able to take part in elementary 'conversations' with an adult partner, usually the mother (Stern, 1977; Trevarthen, 1995). Studies of babies also show an early predisposition to attend to objects and events. Ingenious experiments with newborn babies show that, when supported so that their arms are free, they reach out towards objects (Bower, 1974, 1982). Other studies suggest that newborns quickly form expectations about the movements of objects (Spelke, 1985; 1990). Some psychologists think this is evidence for the existence of internal representations or 'software' present within the baby's brain before birth. They think this means that when the baby is born, she already has primitive ideas about objects and events, and plans for actions. However, there are problems with the idea of innate ideas. Other writers suggest a continuous and dynamic process in which, instead of representations preformed in the brain before birth, perceptual systems already have a history of development in the womb. After birth, these systems start operating in the physical and interpersonal environment, triggered and driven by certain preferences or 'values' (Thelen and Smith, 1994). As I mentioned in the last chapter, these systems seem to capture what things are and where they are.

Newborn babies are interested in the shape, form and movement of objects. Later, these interests will be represented in various media. We have already seen an example of this in Ben's painting about the 'car going around the corner'.

Conversations with newborn babies

The work of Stern (1977) and Trevarthen (1980) shows babies taking part in exquisitely orchestrated conversations with parents, involving facial expression, vocalisation and gesture. The conversations are by no means controlled by the adult partner alone. The baby contributes significantly in setting the theme, pace and tempo, and does not simply adapt to and copy existing behaviours. As in any conversation, each partner has to contribute, otherwise there is no conversation! Babies play a part in the 'creation of culture' (Trevarthen and Grant, 1979, p. 566).

Watching video recordings, frame by frame or in extreme slow motion, of our daughter Hannah (from only a few days old) together with Linda, her mother, reveals a beautiful 'interactional synchrony' (Condon, 1975) of vocalisation, facial expressions and gestures. Mothers and fathers cannot be trained in this interaction – it is natural to them. As Stephen Pinker writes, no parent teaches their babies to speak, they listen carefully to what babies are trying to tell them (Pinker, 1994). Babies control a network of behaviours which are co-ordinated by emotional states of mind (Trevarthen, 1984). One has the sense that mother and baby are brought together in a common purpose or shared act of understanding (Trevarthen and Hubley, 1978; Trevarthen, 1995). Trevarthen has suggested that the baby and caregiver are able to converse because each is able to synchronise her own rhythmical patterns with those of her partner (Trevarthen, 1984; 1995). We will see how these early patterned games, sensitively supported by the caregiver, are gradually developed to include toys, drawing and writing materials.

An emotional space between caregiver and baby

It is within this 'bubble' or psychological space (Stern, 1977, p. 29) formed between partners (caregiver and baby) that actions and then objects come to acquire special meanings. When Linda causes objects to enter this space, they are carefully introduced into Hannah's lines of sight and eye focus. Linda plays and replays her actions in slow motion, carefully adjusting speed and position to what she perceives to be Hannah's ability to look at, and 'track', an object. Piaget suggested that before a baby can communicate with another person, certain basic understandings have to be formed about both objects and space. Trevarthen has suggested that it might be the other way around, that skills in the handling and manipulation of objects could be the result (not the cause) of a baby being able to communicate. In other words, the way babies think and feel about objects and their movements may come about because of the way they communicate with people who are important to them (Vygotsky, 1986). This would suggest that object-mastery is already suffused with emotional and expressive qualities. Gradually, these acts of interpersonal communication become structured in space and time to become games which seem to be universal. A good example, is Joel playing 'peepo' with his daughter (my granddaughter), Keira, when she was six months old. Here, the elements of the game, hiding, disappearance, reappearance, will form the basis of her paintings and drawing and symbolic play in a year's time:

Joel props Keira up slightly, 20 degrees out of the horizontal, on her back on the settee. He sits next to her. She is holding up a purple balloon close to her face. She is holding on to the balloon with both hands, each palm pressed to left or right side of the balloon. Joel also holds on to the balloon, helping maintain it in this position. He hides his head behind the other side of the balloon, softly calling out, 'Keira'. This is a game she knows. She even looks up at the top of the balloon in expectation of his face appearing there. Then Joel pulls the balloon longitudinally away from her and slightly downwards, and looks over the top, saying 'Peepo!' As the balloon is pulled away from her, Keira momentarily tracks its recession, but then she quickly inclines her head upward and sees him, looming over the top of the balloon (see Figure 7). She smiles widely. He does it a second time. By the second time, she is already quite excited and is actively assisting in hiding herself behind the balloon – not merely allowing herself to be hidden – but pulling the balloon towards herself. She moans softly against the balloon, pressing her open mouth up against it, with Joel on the other side. She even raises her eye-gaze up to the top of the balloon in expectation of his appearing there. She kicks her feet and gives a little gurgling shriek, her excitement mounting. He appears over the top of the balloon again, saying, 'Peepo!' She looks up at him, opens her mouth in a big smile, her eyes widening. By the fourth time, she kicks her legs in excitement as she hides behind the balloon. During the fifth, sixth and seventh time, she is panting and she makes increasingly louder, gurgling laughs as she awaits Joel's reappearance. After the third 'peepo' of this new series, she is kicking her feet excitedly. On the fourth go, instead of putting his face over the top, Joel puts his head underneath the balloon. Keira does not seem unduly surprised but seems to quickly adjust her eye-gaze, although – perhaps significantly – her smile is not quite so wide. When Joel appears underneath the balloon the next time, she is ready for this, immediately turning her eye-gaze downward. Joel resumes appearing over the top of the balloon and after the seventh 'peepo' of this series she is actually laughing. Joel continues 17 times, Keira's laughter becoming increasingly hysterical, with perhaps a note of anxiety entering into it by the end of the play.

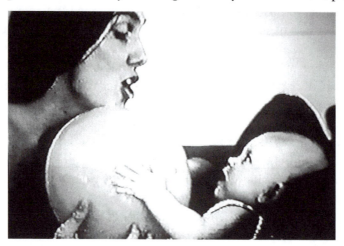

Figure 7   Joel and Keira

Analysis and discussion

Keira anticipates what Joel is going to do. She readies herself for the game. She assists Joel in moving the balloon to the correct position. She seems to display an understanding of the timing involved. When there is a pause in the game and Joel starts to talk to me, moving the balloon slightly away from her to the side, she actually grasps the balloon with her palms on each side and pulls it back into position. Not only does she help hold the balloon in place, a more subtle indication of her understanding of the game is that, at that moment when the balloon completely obstructs her view of Joel's face, she also averts her eye-gaze downward, looking into the balloon, preparing herself for the surprise of seeing his face, actively engaging in building up the suspense. Joel pushes the play to the limits of her excitement. He can do this because his understanding of her, and hers of him, is so intimate and complete. If a stranger attempted the same play with Keira she would probably be distressed.

Drawing and painting start within such bubbles of space formed between caregiver and child. How the adult interprets and responds to what the child does is crucial to the child's emergent representation and expression. Clearly, language is part of this and so is the way the caregiver responds, in every way, to the child's speech. There is nothing extraordinary about Joel and Keira in this way. Most adults, especially parents, seem to like getting into conversations with babies, and most babies seem to be able to respond. There are some important implications here about childcare and education which will be followed up at the end of this chapter.

The timing, tempo and cadence of these conversations between baby and caregiver become a dynamic pattern for later play, from which acts of representation and expression with material things will be constructed. Condon's (1975) work showed that talking to babies makes them move. The movement of their arms, legs and faces occurs in bursts which are linked with their parent's utterances. If a person makes objects move within the baby's visual field, this also brings about bursts of movement from the baby. Perhaps this is because adults imbue the object with human-type actions. In their experiments, Martin Richards and his colleagues found that babies responded differently to jerky, irregular movement and predictable, regular, mechanical movements in rolling ball-bearings they were shown. Richards thought that irregular movements might be similar to human movements and were therefore particularly interesting to babies (Richards, 1980). Additionally, the movements and visual transformations of objects made to penetrate the interpersonal space between infant and caregiver take on the movements of the human agencies who propel them, and so become loaded with emotional significance and emergent representational values.

Filmed and video-recorded observations made during her first weeks of life show Hannah participating with enthusiasm in events occurring within this bubble of space between her and her caregiver. At four days old, she probably cannot see clearly more than about 20–70 cm, and she prefers to look at things which are very close to her face. But though this is a small bubble of space, what happens within it is very powerful to her – especially if it involves movements, of her own arms and legs, and the close-up hand, arm and facial actions of her caregiver. Moreover, anything she can see, she can probably also reach (Eliot, 1999).

As I bend over her while she lies on her back, Hannah makes rhythmical arm and leg movements towards me. The movements she makes are almost circular, alternating from one arm to the other. Each movement is a little like a crawl swimming stroke. These actions have been observed by other writers, including Gesell (1946) and Thelen and Smith (1994). In response to the attention or the speech of an adult caregiver, the baby makes actions involving the legs, arms, fingers and facial muscles. It may be that such movements of the body are articulated according to a linguistic basis shared also with early drawing actions. It may be the case that all forms of representation, be they pictorial, written or spoken, share the same basis in the actions of the body (Allott, 2001).

Very often the fingers, too, are involved, moving through intricate oscillations. The same can be observed when children begin to paint and draw. As we shall see, early drawing and painting involve many movements, not only those of the drawing hand. Drawing actions are discovered from earlier actions. Sometimes it is as though the child is acting out a story, event or image, just as people use gestures of the hands, arms and face when in conversation with each other. Yet, aside from actions of the drawing hand itself, most researchers of children's drawing ignore all other movements made by children, assuming them irrelevant or even disruptive to drawing proper. Yet it is a mistake to think of drawing and painting in such a narrow, simplistic way. Drawing is discovered from a background of other actions that the baby can already produce. The earliest drawing actions are based upon early gesticulations of the body already articulated into emotional and expressive phrases and passages. Hence, the first drawings made with a marking instrument of some kind already have a history to them. In developmental terms, it is meaningless to seek the precise moment when 'real' drawing begins.

The players imitate and extend each other's movements. What is perhaps surprising is the precision of the baby, whose movements alternate with those of the partner with a fine sense of timing. The baby is not merely copying; rather, the baby plays a strong part in initiating these games and in controlling their intensity and length. By around two years of age, Hannah initiates, with a parent, games which involve rhythmical patterns of hand movements, feet stampings or hand slappings, with a single slap of her hand.

Later, we will see how Hannah develops these games, so that by the age of two, it includes painting processes, in beautifully co-ordinated, rhythmic sequences of action, sensitively supported by Linda, her mother.

Looking at filmed and video-recorded observations of Hannah and her mother show that, once the games have started, it is sometimes hard to work out who is the leader and who is the follower. The sensitive parent responds to subtle movements of the baby imitating, repeating and extending them. In a way, the adult makes a continuous 'commentary' on the baby's actions (Harris, 1989, p. 22). A conversation is created, made up of vocalisation, facial expression and gestures.

Babies and movement

Being able to produce one's own movements is fundamental to perception and understanding. Even though the movements of the baby may, at first, seem uncontrolled, nevertheless the baby receives perceptual feedback about her surroundings and her own relationship to it. Babies become aware of their own movements. At fourteen days old, Hannah catches sight of her own fist as it flies past her face. She tracks its trajectory as she would that of any other moving object. It may be that she does not at first realise the fist is her own. It may be that initially babies are unaware that they themselves cause their bodies to move. Realising that there is a relationship between our own actions and their effects is the basis for later expression and representation.

Soon, babies seem to move their arms, fingers and legs as if for the sole purpose of studying these movements. By the age of two months, for example, Hannah holds her hand in front of her face, gently rotating it back and forth on its axis. She studies it intently. It is no longer a question of her catching sight of her fist as it fortuitously zips across her field of vision. She is now able to hold her hand steady in front of her eyes in order to move it and look at it. She moves her hand away from her and, at the moment of furthest reach, gracefully fans out her fingers. It is as if she is breaking down actions into their component units and analysing them. She also bangs her palm against surfaces and then holds her hand before her eyes and gazes at it with interest (Bower, 1974, 1982; White, Castle and Held, 1964; Thelen and Smith, 1994; Thelen et al., 2000).

Three basic movements of the hand and arm will be useful to Hannah when she begins to draw. These actions derive from the most natural oscillations and swayings of the skeletal and muscular frame (Smith, 1983). I have called them *vertical arc*, *horizontal arc* and *push-pull* (Matthews, 1983; 1984; 1999). (See Figures 4, 5 and 6.) The way each develops is complex. The development of each action can be described separately but it is important to appreciate that they are members of a family and that they interact with each other.

Perceptual mapping is set in motion whenever the infant moves, co-ordinating movements of the body, touch and visual perception. These different systems are mapped onto each other during time and, combined together, give the infant 'knowledge' about her surroundings and her relationship to it. As we have seen, babies are interested in where things are, what things are and how they move from place to place. They will also try to keep interesting objects within sight and reach out to them. Trying to keep an object in sight helps exercise visual tracking. As with all other actions performed by the child within the environment, the acts of reaching towards objects and trying to grasp them create further opportunities for exploration which will require the formation of new motor skills. In turn, these new motor actions will open up further possibilities for interaction, requiring the design of further skills, and so on. In this way, a loop of interaction is formed in which what the child discovers in one context sets the scene for new ways of interacting with the world.

The baby has a variety of waving, fanning, and flapping movements, up and down, and side to side. Gradually, babies learn to control their own muscular torque (the natural, elastic tensions of the muscular and skeletal systems which tend to hold the body in certain positions) and compensate for the effects of gravity in order to get the hand within the vicinity of interesting objects. The child will differentiate the actions into generalised categories which will become useful, multipurpose strategies for contacting objects, investigating surfaces and as communicative gestures.

Three movements will be useful to Hannah when she begins to draw. These are, making a vertical arc, a horizontal arc and a push-pull (Matthews, 1983; 1984; 1994; 1999; 2002 in press). The way each develops is complex. The development of each action can be described separately but it is important to appreciate that they are members of a family and that they interact with each other.

Vertical arc

The vertical arc is linked with the way a baby understands an object or person as something to use as a target. Hannah is sixteen days old. A multicoloured cube is presented within her visual field. She swipes at the cube with a downwards, circular action. People are targeted in the same way. A few days later,

Hannah smiles excitedly when Joel approaches and plays with her. She swipes her hand excitedly in vertical arcs towards him. These early movements are put to different uses but are all equally important. For example, babies test and investigate objects and surfaces by striking them, and they reach out towards people. Some of their reaching movements are adapted to become the beginnings of pointing out objects to other people. It can also be used as an excited response to the appearance of people who are important to the baby. This movement also forms part of a rhythmical game with a partner. The vertical arc may be used in rhythmical games involving stampings and beatings of the hands and/or feet. Later (as in the observation of Ben in Chapter 1) this action may be used with a marking instrument to make dots, blobs or spots.

There are some important teaching implication here about the kind and quality of support which might foster children's development and learning. These will be mentioned at the end of this chapter. Because these early movements are used for communication as well as for mastery of objects, the movements are saturated with emotion. This has consequences later in this child's life when they are applied to drawing and painting.

Horizontal arc

Vertical and horizontal arcs are interwoven as they develop and become basic mark-making movements. The vertical arc develops fairly rapidly over the first and second months; for swiping at objects, for outward reach and grasp and, like the vertical arc, as an excited response to people she knows. Sometimes this looks like the beginning of an embrace. But the horizontal arc only really begins to develop as an expressive and representational strategy when the baby can be propped up to sit and reach horizontal surfaces. For Hannah, this occurs at about three months of age. She uses it as a fanning or wiping gesture, usually across smooth, horizontal surfaces. She also makes semi-circular arcs back and forth in front of the middle of her chest. This is an early form of the movement Ben uses at age two years and one month with a brush, to start the painting process I described in Chapter 1.

The following observation is from slow-motion film recordings of Hannah: Hannah is three months old and she sits in her little chair, with her meal tray before her. She sweeps her hand across her tray towards a wooden rattle. Sometimes, using this action, she knocks the rattle onto the floor.

She is beginning to build up knowledge about the relationships between objects and the surfaces upon which they rest, as well as her knowledge of her own movements. One interesting discovery is that objects can be slid and scattered along and off horizontal surfaces. For this manoeuvre, she learns to use the horizontal arc. She finds she can gather up and capture objects too. Of course, it is also possible to disperse objects so that they are out of reach but visible from a different viewpoint, or even to lose objects, when they are scattered out of sight. These understandings will be combined together to form a larger and more encompassing understanding of the movement, shape and location of objects and one's relationship to them. Such under-standings are behind the making of many art forms.

Typically, a parent will offer an object to a baby at around the centre of the baby's chest. When objects are dangled around this 'hot-spot' as it has been termed (Gray, 1978, p. 168), the baby will look at it and at her hands and then her hands will then close in upon it from both sides. Hannah, at three months and four days, is lying on her back. An object is dangled at the centre of her chest and she moves her arms towards it at this central 'hot-spot'. Nineteen days later, she uses horizontal and vertical arcs in three ways:

- to contact objects;
- to gather objects;
- to scatter objects.

In particular, Hannah has developed an all-purpose downward striking movement which she applies with gusto to a range of objects and surfaces. Hannah keeps modifying her movements depending on where the object is. We can see her using her own body as a landmark. This helps her to control the natural swingings and stabbings of her arm and hand by relating these movements to her central 'hot-spot'. It takes excruciating concentration. Sometimes she manages to control the way her hands meet in front of her chest so that they clasp each other, and occasionally manages to clasp the desired object. She clearly takes great pleasure in her success.

Later, we will see how 'landmarks', such as the position of an object, and parts of the body, become co-ordinated and begin to play an important part in early drawings and paintings.

Push-pull

The push-pull, the last of the trio of mark-making gestures, does not really make an appearance until the fourth month, because the baby must be able to grasp an object. Babies need to understand the difference between reaching and grasping in order to hold pencils, brushes and so on, and to draw and paint.

This means that, before looking in detail at 'push-pull' movements, it is necessary to make a detour in order to consider how the baby develops reaching and grasping skills.

Reaching and grasping

According to recent studies, reaching and grasping is a multimodal assembly of systems within specific contexts (Thelen and Smith, 1994; Thelen et al., 2000). Reaching is discovered from a history of movements the baby has already acquired. Grasping an object can be achieved in many ways but the infant selects and uses an action pattern from her own individual repertoire. As with all other actions, this has great developmental and learning significance. Again we notice that, although to a certain extent development seems predictable and orderly, with certain skills achieved at approximately the same age, the way each course of development runs is unique to that individual. In the case of reaching and grasping, although the end result – reaching and grasping the object – is generally achieved at about the same age, the route to this end point varies. Each child's development journey will be unique because each individual's muscular and skeletal framework is unique and the ways in which these systems interact with the world will be different. That each child finds individual solutions for skills has enormous implications for the way we provide for and support learning experiences.

Babies try hard to analyse and correct their movements. We have already seen, earlier in this chapter, that they find their own movements and the results of these interesting. Here is another example.

Hannah, aged two years and nine days, is lying quietly in bed on her back. In the absence of any object, she makes repeated reaching and grasping movements while intently watching her hand. She holds her closed fist close to her face for a moment, studying it. The elbow is bent in this position. Then she moves her fist away from her, using an overarm arc. At the end of its trajectory, the arm is outstretched while the fingers gracefully fan out. She does this dozens of times, watching with a rapt expression. Hannah seems to be repeating the separate movements of reaching and grasping without an object. We see her taking apart sequences of action as if to analyse them and gain complete understanding and mastery of them. We will see this careful monitoring and adjustment of actions again and again.

The slow-motion films made of her when she was about four months old show her developing and analysing the skills involved in picking up and holding an object. In slow motion, we see she adjusts the position of her fingers and palm in mid-flight to fit the shape of the object she wants to hold. This 'in-flight' correction is an important achievement (Bower, 1974, 1982, p. 175). Hannah is practising, analysing and co-ordinating patterns of action of looking, reaching and grasping. These are fundamental skills for the use of tools, such as pencils and brushes. They will be useful for drawing and painting later on.

Horizontal arc and push-pull used in painting

In the observation with which we started, when Ben paints, he combines the horizontal arc, vertical arc and push-pull. He starts his painting with a back and forth horizontal arcing of the brush, but he soon alternates this action with a push-pull movement. Like the horizontal arc, the push-pull requires him to make an arm and hand movement along a flat, usually horizontal, plane. Ben has to adapt his movements because the push-pull involves the use of the elbow. The push-pull is usually made with an object on a surface. Ben holds a paintbrush and paints onto paper on the table. The push-pull is therefore a more advanced movement. It joins the other two movements, vertical arc and horizontal arc, to complete the trio of early drawing actions, when objects can be held in the hand and manipulated.

The push-pull is not glimpsed in Hannah's movements until she is about three months old, when she is learning to push and pull objects along flat, smooth, horizontal surfaces. At age three months and four days, using two hands, she holds a bowl by a section of the rim nearest her and pushes it to and from herself along the surface of the table, in sudden bursts of action. Over the next few days and weeks she learns the difference between 'push' and 'pull' and finds important uses for each. Thirteen days later, for example, she can push her bowl away from her or pull it towards her – whichever she wants.

Because children find the effects of their movements interesting, they repeat and develop them. They start to match movements to various materials. In effect, babies select on the basis of suiting their own purposes. For example, the push-pull is particularly effective with a wheeled toy. At five months old, Hannah repeatedly pushes and pulls a little wooden, wheeled dog to and from herself on the floor.

Near the end of his painting act, Ben repeatedly stabs downwards, using the vertical arc, making red spots appear inside the blue closure formed when he enacted the car's elliptical journey. He then finishes the painting episode by obliterating this image by the wiping action of the energetic horizontal arc.

Summary

From birth, babies create a family of strategies with which they investigate objects and surfaces. They gradually begin to reach and grasp, swipe and fan, and in doing so obtain different effects. As the months pass, they learn to adapt these actions to suit different needs. It is not enough to describe this process in terms of object-mastery alone, because the sequences into which the baby organises her actions form expressive phrases. This expressive aspect happens when the baby is on her own but is especially promoted in inter-personal contexts. The baby employs movement in playful exchanges with people, and in order to communicate with them. This means that the baby's actions are invested with a range of emotional values. Movements are given meaning in a joint enterprise of child and adult companion. Recent research has suggested that the baby's gestures are a kind of language upon which other forms of representation, including writing, speech and drawing, are soon based. This language is not an arbitrary system of signs but, along with other forms of representation, including drawing, is based upon actions of the body which are already grammatically and semantically articulated – that is, this gestural language already has organisation and meaning. This is the opposite of the conventional wisdom that drawing (and writing and speech) are achieved by training the initially disorganised body into a set or system of arbitrary signs. According to this traditional approach, essentially haphazard natural actions come to attain meaning only when they have been sacrificed or abandoned in favour of a 'corrected' sequence.

The beginning of painting and drawing

The beginning of marking actions will be revealed to be far different from the 'scribbling stage' of conventional theory. Rather, the child engages in an investigation of visual and dynamic structure in its own right while at the same time discerning the expressive and representational possibilities of mark-making. The concept of *play* is important here because it is the main mechanism with which children temporarily liberate actions and objects from the confines of adaptation, allowing investigation of processes as entities of interest in themselves and worthy of repetition. These early visual and sensory experiences shape the emergent mind (Eliot, 1999). If you think about it, the argument is not about how much such activities contribute to intelligence, nor whether or not 'art' is important in education. Asking such questions is absurd. Intelligence itself is built upon that which we crudely term 'children's art'.

3

The beginning of painting and drawing

Three dimensions – objects and people

Chapter 2 showed that development and learning are not passive processes but involve babies in actively searching the environment for the experiences which will help them as they grow. We have seen how the baby creates a set or family of strategies with which to investigate all kinds of objects and surfaces. This interest existed at birth. Depending on the object, and the movement used to investigate it (reaching and grasping, or swiping and fanning), different effects are obtained. The range of objects explored and contacted is great, including objects which are clearly three dimensional; objects which, when struck, might roll or tumble, or perhaps fall and break. Throughout these investigations, babies adapt their actions in the light of what happens. Piaget called this process *accommodation*. For example, Hannah learns to set overturned toys upright with guided pull and grasp. Another explanation is that a new 'attractor system' is being formed from new experiences. This system will be mapped over earlier systems and, combined together, gradually will form a new, dynamic category of knowledge.

Two dimensions

Babies also investigate other objects which are not so clearly three-dimensional. These include very flat objects on flat surfaces. Babies can be seen to be studying and scratching at small specks and spots of material. They can be surprisingly adept at picking up miniscule items like hairs. In this way, babies gain a great deal of knowledge about surfaces, boundaries and volumes of objects. Of course, this only happens if babies have opportunities for self-motivated exploration. Being able to roll over, being able to lift one's head when lying on one's stomach; such newly acquired skills mark the beginnings of new universes of perceptual and action possibilities.

Self-initiated and self-directed movement in the environment provide the infant with major information about the structure of objects and events. As movement becomes extended, by crawling, and later walking, so new vistas, literally and metaphorically, open up. These, in turn, provide opportunities for further discoveries about the nature of the environment and the objects and events which occur within it.

Babies are also attracted to things they see which cannot actually be picked up at all. These include pictures. Bower (1974, 1982) has claimed that children are not fooled by pictures, and it is certainly true that they do not behave as if these were real objects. Nevertheless, my own observations show that babies reach towards two-dimensional images as if to grasp them. I speculate that, although they might realise that these are in fact ungraspable, they are compelled to explore the characteristics of pictures with the patterns of action they have available to them. In my studies, the babies, after scratching at the edges of the picture and finding no physical change, will then move their hands out to the edges of the pages of the book or the picture as if to locate the true boundaries of the object.

First painting

Joel, at just over six months, is lying on his stomach on a purple carpet. He regurgitates some milk onto the carpet in front of him, presenting a contrasting, white, circular patch before his eyes. He reaches his fingers into this irresistible visual target and makes a scratching movement. He hears his fingers scratching into the carpet and he seems to be interested in the changes he is causing to take place.

Hannah and Ben also searched small pools of spilt milk, locating edges and boundaries. Such behaviour might appear trivial (or even unpleasant) to some people but there are several important aspects to be considered here. Joel has modified his movements. Finding milk ungraspable, he has modified his grasping to a scratching motion.

When a baby begins the scratching movement, a trace of milk is left behind. This is unique to the situation where the baby is using a mark-making substance, like paint, or in this case, milk! It leaves a record of the baby's action. The baby realises that he or she has the power to create changes in the environment.

The fact that actions, perhaps initiated with the purpose of grasping an object, result in a completely novel, visual phenomenon, creates another developmental dimension. It leads to visual expression and representation. Hence, movement initially designed to accommodate to objects forms a new category of movement designed and developed for expressive purposes.

The beginning of painting and drawing, then, occupies a unique place in a baby's life. It offers the baby lasting information about the characteristics of his or her movements in space. First, the trails present a visual guide for actions originally executed for object-mastery. But there is more to it than this. Because the results of the actions are so novel, they set in train a quite new developmental pathway. They offer the baby powerful expressive possibilities. The baby perceives a relationship between the actions she makes, the mood she makes them in and the resultant trace.

We have seen in the observations of Hannah and Ben that they are beginning to make this relationship – they realise that movement results in a mark. Ben goes on to understand that the character or precise shape of the mark made is a result of a combination of factors including the characteristic of the movement and the possibilities (and limitations) of the medium. For example, making an action in splashy milk will feel different, and look different from making the same kind of action in thick, gooey paint. The possibilities are multiplied still further when a tool is used. The baby begins to guide painting and drawing according to the marks he or she sees occurring. It is this intense feedback, unique to drawing and painting, which helps the baby put different movements together in new ways. Eventually, this process will allow the baby to consciously produce different shapes.

Realising that movements make marks

Initially the baby makes marks with his or her hands (and sometimes feet) in various liquids. At around the same time (perhaps eight months) the baby might notice an interesting effect caused by dashing certain kinds of objects against surfaces. These objects are mark-making instruments of various kinds. They leave marks in their wake as they travel along surfaces – the 'trace-making effects' described by Michotte (1963, p. 289). The baby looks carefully at the points of these instruments and discovers which positions and movements of the marker against the mark-receiving surface make interesting effects on it. She experiments with various actions and relationships of marker to surface, clearly in order to establish how the marks are made

(Smith, 1983; Matthews, 1999), when the marks appear and when they fail to appear. Sometimes the baby slides a pencil along on its side, or presses its non-drawing end against the surface. The baby is very interested in the marks produced by bare hands and those produced by drawing tools.

The baby has understood the most basic principle of drawing, which is that a movement results in a mark. Soon after, the baby starts to realise that different actions result in different effects. Earlier on, the baby investigated and analysed objects, finding out about their shape and form, and what made them move. Now, the structure of marks, and the movements which make them, are also investigated and analysed.

In the early days, paint is to be slapped, smeared, stamped and sat in! Ben, sitting on the floor at the age of one year and four months, paints with a brush, on the floor and all around his own body (Matthews, 1983). To a certain extent, the first location or landmark around which painting is orientated, is one's own body. However, the beginnings of painting and drawing are not just a reflection of the natural actions of the body. The brush, an object, forces the toddler to modify and change her actions. So does the surface it is used upon. The object (three-dimensional) now meets a surface (two-dimensional) and makes marks (two-dimensional) upon it. This calls for some fine-tuning of the drawing actions, but some children have made these modifications by the end of their first year.

Horizontal arc

Joel, at thirteen months of age, has learned to toddle. He also likes to carry his cup of milk around with him. However, co-ordinating these two new skills is not easy and he frequently spills milk. On one occasion, the milk falls onto a smooth, shiny concrete floor. Joel, his jaw dripping, watches with great interest the spreading white shape. He then puts his right hand into the milk and starts to smear it, using the horizontal arcing motion. He quickly brings his other hand into play, so that both hands are fanning to and fro in synchrony, meeting at the mid-line, until they become out of phase. In this way, he makes two sectors of a circle in the split milk (see Figures 8, 9 and 10).

It is important to realise that Joel's recently acquired skill in walking has, in itself, literally and metaphorically opened up new vistas for him. Such achievements signal not only what the child can do but more a change in the child's relationship with the world (Costall, 1992, personal communication). It also testifies to the importance of self-locomotion, showing how

Figure 8   Joel spills milk from his cup

Figure 9   He reaches into the spilt milk

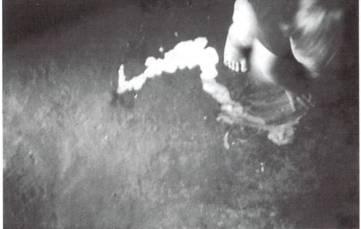

Figure 10   He makes horizontal arcs in the milk, using both hands

achievements in perception, cognition and action are interrelated systems stimulated and driven by self-initiated and self-directed movement. Each new achievement sets in motion new sequences of movement along new avenues of development. In addition to being able to walk, Joel can now walk towards things he can see from a distance, and he can bend over to study them or pick them up or sit down and handle them. Dramatic changes in perception happen in these landmark moments in development. One example, is when my granddaughter, Poppy, manages to sit upright on her bottom, instead of being restricted to supine, prone positions on either back or stomach. As soon as she can sit up, the visual scene and its opportunities are vastly changed and so further developments occur in hot pursuit. These developments include visually searching the environment and learning to reach and take hold of something.

Joel begins to draw and paint

I have suggested that the apparent 'accidental' nature of children's early painting may, in many accounts, have been overemphasised. There is nothing accidental about Joel's horizontal arc in the milk at thirteen months. He has already passed through the struggle of mastering this and can now perform this action in a number of contexts. However, no sooner has he mastered the action than he has to make adjustments to it, because the new situations immediately demand modifications be made to the mark.

A good example is three weeks later when he uses a brush and orange paint to make a horizontal arcing trace on my studio floor. Before, he used the palm of his hand in milk to make his arc, now it has been extended or 'amplified' to use Jerome Bruner's (1964) term because he is using a brush. He tries all sorts of movement with the brush to get to know its possibilities. First, crouching on his haunches, he waves the brush in an arc in the air, causing droplets to fly off. The filmed observations show Joel carefully looking at the trail of droplets as they make an arc on the floor. Perhaps finding himself unsteady in this position, he stands up. This seems to prompt a different movement – a vigorous stabbing motion of the brush in the air. This is a version of the vertical arc which meets empty space rather than a surface. Again, droplets of paint cascade onto the floor. There is definitely nothing accidental about this; Joel knows what he is doing. He knows that milk can be spurted from the spout of the shaken cup and uses this knowledge with the brush and paint. My detailed recorded observations show that Joel chooses,

Figure 11 Joel uses grasping and tasting actions to test the new objects and media

Figure 12 Joel quickly discovers the marking potential of paint. He paints his own body with his finger

Figure 13 Joel tries to put a big brush into a small pot. He is finding out about inside and outside relationships

Figure 14 Joel discovers the uses of a brush. He paints his toenails red

Figure 15 Joel makes a horizontal arc on the floor using a brush. A few days before, he had made this kind of action with his hands

Figure 16 Joel pours yellow paint onto the floor. He is finding out about inside and outside relationships, emptying and emptiness

from a whole set of possibilities, a single expressive movement. Joel knows when to use it, how to use it and what it is good for. (See Figures 11 to 16.)

Between thirteen and fourteen months old, Joel keeps repeating vertical and horizontal arcing movements. Because we know that Joel at this time has a range of options available to him, we can be fairly certain that when he reaches into the milk, or applies the brush to the floor, he does so with the intention of making that movement.

Reasons not causes

To be sure, in many instances, especially when the paint is dripped or splashed, the exact nature and location of the splashes of paint cannot be predicted, but by far and away the more important point is that *he knows this too*. He has learnt this technique in earlier spillings of liquid – milk for example. He now sets up a situation precisely in order to obtain some chance results. By observing the results, this will inform him about further possibilities of expressive action. Here, I am invoking a far different idea of chance and accident than the one of traditional accounts of development. What we loosely call chance or accident are part of a complex interaction between the child, his intentions and their effects in the world.

Summary

Between the ages of one and two years of age, children form knowledge about the world and the objects and events which occur within it. The main way they are able to gain this knowledge is by self-initiated and self-directed movement within the environment. Movement must itself be considered a basic form of perception (Thelen and Smith, 1994; Thelen et al., 2000). As the ways of moving around the environment change, so the child's knowledge of the shape and form of objects and events change. Each new discovery offers up a new range of possibilities, and so on. It is not a stage-like process, but a seamless continuum and each child's journey through this developmental landscape is unique.

A crucial part of this development is the child's realisation that her actions have an effect on the world. She can make a difference to it. The most dramatic way the child realises this is when she draws. It is only through drawing that the infant receives a record of her movements. Anna Stetsenko argues that drawing is a child's first introduction to semiotic systems (symbols and signs, like writing, numbers and pictures). This is because, in drawing, the child dramatically perceives what Vygotsky referred to as the dual function of symbols and signs; that while a mark is just a mark, at the same time it can can stand for (represent) something quite other than itself. This is the 'double knowledge' crucial for the basis of symbol and sign use (Furth, 1969). Perhaps in no other expressive and/or representational medium is it so clearly demonstrated.

In the observations I have discussed, the child is right at the beginning of this process. The baby is beginning to understand the connection between certain movements and certain marks. Part of this development is made possible because of the ways in which pencils and brushes, in the hands of young children, make chance collisions. Even uncontrolled movements record important visual, postural, haptic and kinaesthetic information through co-operation of perceptual systems. This information sets up a continuous and seamless flow of actions constantly retuned in response to what is made visible.

It appears that babies purposely seek out accidents, searching for ways which might cause new effects to occur. These understandings are combined with prior discoveries to form more complex actions. It is a continuous 'conversation', sometimes called a 'dialectical' relationship, between the acting, thinking, feeling child, her intentions and their effects in the world.

Children are naturally interested in marks and movements for their own sake, as well as their representational possibilities. Children will alternate between representational concerns and visual and dynamic structure independent of representation and meaning. They will 'free-flow' between these concerns (Bruce, 1991). Dennie Wolf (1989) suggests that speech, movement and marks 'speak' to each other. When very young children paint, it is a truly chaotic act, but only in the recent sense of the term, in that the apparent turbulence conceals substructures of highly organised, patterned sequences and periodicities, as Bruce (1991) states with regards to play. Clearly, it is essential for teaching and childcare how we identify and illuminate the nature of this order within chaos.

4

Movement into shape

Separating and combining movement and shapes

Before their second birthday, most children have already learnt that different movements make different shapes. For example, at twenty-one months Ben uses very different movements to make contrasts between shapes. He uses existing marks or lines on the paper as targets. He often dissects these, drawing arcs or push-pulls across them. Or else, he clusters dots or blobs at the beginnings or ends of lines (see Figure 17). The beginnings and ends of lines are important landmarks for children of this age and will continue to be so as they grow older (Athey, 1990; Matthews, 1999). Hannah also clusters marks at the beginnings and ends of lines, or groups dots and dashes around angles formed by arcing or push-pulling movements (see Figures 18 and 19). Perhaps such structures form the basis of human vision (Costall, 1993; 1995). This may be the reason babies visually attend to patterns in human faces (Bower, 1974, 1982; Thelen and Smith, 1994; Atkinson, 2002 forthcoming).

Figure 17 Ben, aged one year and nine months, makes contrasting painting movements. Blobs are clustered at the ends of lines

*Figure 18   Hannah, aged two
years and two months, clusters
blobs at the ends of lines*

*Figure 19   Hannah, aged
two years and four months,
clusters marks at the ends
of lines. 'I show Mummy,'
she says*

Although newborn vision is blurred, looming, moving, close-up faces are very interesting to babies. They may first discern the overall closure of the face; later, the interior features, mouth, eyes and nose. They attend to contrasts of light intensity and texture, and variations in the shapes in and around the mother's eyes. This sequence may be reiterated when, later on (around two years), the infant draws closed shapes followed by the placing of marks inside closed shapes.

The formation of lines and shapes and colours they see on the painting or drawing surface 'tell' Ben and Hannah something about the world. Recent work on computer vision also supports this idea (Costall, 1993; 1995). Using John Willats's theory of early topological geometry, computer programmes have been designed which produce childlike drawings (Burton, 1997; Whale, 2002; Tormey and Whale, 2002).

Ben, at this time responds to, and learns to create, other dramatic contrasts of direction. He likes to make angles and lines which cut through, or even bisect, other lines. He likes to put lines against dots or blobs. The basic movements of his hand and arm as he draws are the horizontal arc, the push-pull and the vertical arc.

A family of shapes

Children become increasingly attracted to making angular and criss-cross shapes. These shapes often emerge as early as one year of age, and are certainly very clear in paintings and drawings produced by Ben, Joel and Hannah from eighteen months of age (see Figures 20 and 21). In paintings by children at this time, horizontal arcing movements suddenly change direction as the painting arm pulls the brush back towards the body. This is the start of a family of shapes. Children begin to separate out and to classify lines and actions. This is the beginning of behaviours and understandings which can truly be defined as mathematical.

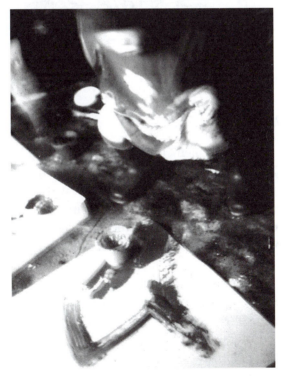

Figure 20   Joel, eighteen months old, makes right-angular turns *in a brush line ...*

Figure 21 ... and develops right-angular structure

Push and pull

At about eighteen months Ben, Joel and Hannah begin to separate push actions from pull actions. Sometimes this results in single lines on the paper. These are the beginnings of vertical lines but I will refer to such lines as 'proto-verticals'. We should be cautious about naming these early, single lines true 'verticals' since they are the result of body movements. However, it is the start of the mapping, onto the drawing surface, of a vertical axis (see Figures 23 and 24).

From about fifteen months Hannah contrasts two arcing movements of the brush – one making a right angle with the other. She makes a different contrast by energetically varying the way she moves her wrist and arm, and yet maintains continuous contact with the paper so that lines join up at angles with the lines already made. This is a pattern of movement which Hannah uses repeatedly up to the age of two. She also makes little star shapes (see Figure 22).

Figure 22   Hannah, aged one year and eleven months, makes little star-like shapes

Children repeat these, and other contrasting combinations, creating variations. Children seem to enjoy sharply alternating between different actions which result in contrasting shapes. The information about the body actions which make the shape are emphasised and reinforced by the resulting contrast between shapes.

The movements are patterned in time as well as in space. As yet we do not know enough about these patterns of movement but it may be that a system for the action pattern (involved with the motor movements) is mapped over another, visual, system (involved with shape detection), thereby deepening a new attractor system in which action and shape are matched.

Making connections

From around two years of age, children start to separate shapes from each other, yet at the same time link them together. This also occurs when the child distinguishes between the marks which appear on paper and the movements which made them. When this happens, new possibilities arise. They can now separate the different parts of lines and shapes, and link and combine them in various ways.

Drawing helps us see and understand

Contrasts in both two- and three-dimensional situations fascinate children. We can see this in Ben, Joel and Hannah between the ages of three and four years, when their interest in right angles alerts them to letter formations they see. This is a part of what has been termed 'developmental' or 'emergent' writing and will be discussed in Chapter 7. The American psychologist James Gibson (1966) proposes the interesting idea that in prehistorical times the act of drawing started and guided a different way of seeing and understanding the world. In everyday life, it is necessary to quickly identify objects, animals and spaces for purely practical purposes or for reasons of survival. Creating pictures meant that people could start to appreciate shape and form for quite different reasons. The same process may have occurred with the use, in painting, of colour. Perception of colour in the environment serves an important survival function because it adds enormously to visual information. Perhaps painting similarly prompted a different understanding and use of colour, which was emotional and expressive; freed from the demands of adaptation.

Using colour: contrasts and links

One of the ways very young children use colour is to 'colour-code' each drawing or painting movement. They might make one painting action in one colour and the next painting action with another colour, and so on. It is as though children feel that each movement and each mark deserves its own special, distinguishing colour. In this way children link movement, shapes and colours. They sometimes synchronise vocalisations to each painting action too – a one-to-one correspondence which has many important implications for logicomathematical and musical understanding as well as visual expression and representation. It is like a game children create about actions and shapes in time and space. As mathematicians will tell you, 'games' are by no means trivial but have embedded within them important, powerful and beautiful mathematical rules (Nasar, 2002).

Such actions-patterns in the organisation of media develop and soon become quite complex. Here is one example of how this development might run. Ben, aged one year and eleven months, finds a piece of A4 size paper which has been folded (by an adult) into four so that, unfolded, the paper is divided into four rectangles by the clear creases. Ben marks each of these rectangles with a different shape. Then, using small, intense arcings of the crayon, he superimposes black, over green, over orange, each additional layer bisecting the previous layer at a contrasting angle. He is actively trying to differentiate and separate things out. This is important when children begin to move into two-dimensional construction. Ben also orchestrates movements with the marks he makes on paper. He notices the effects on his 'targets' as he draws. He covers one layer with another. In Chapter 5, we shall see how this leads to the representation of one object in front of, or behind, another. This will lead to an understanding of what is termed a *projective* relationship, in which a three-dimensional world is mapped onto the two-dimensional surface. Because of a limited definition of drawing, as well as only vaguest idea of perspective and other drawing systems, most researchers do not realise that projective relationships are present in the drawings of very young children.

That Ben targets what he has already drawn means he draws one thing on top of another. Different colours are layered one upon another, and he chooses where. In a felt-tip drawing Hannah, aged two years and one month, chooses the ends of lines. So, in covering one layer of pigment over another, the toddler is starting to bring about and see colour changes taking place. Hannah and Ben are learning to mix colours. Norman Freeman notes that the aiming actions of the very young infant are quite accurate – a finding which may surprise some people (Freeman, 1980). Ben, Joel and Hannah all aim at the mark with great accuracy and, even if the pencil subsequently skids around, the first impact – even at small points – is on target.

The importance of marks and the spaces between them

Sometimes an empty space is chosen as a target for mark-making. Joel, aged eighteen months, produces a series of pull lines, placed side by side. He carefully separates nearly every line from its neighbour with a gap (see Figure 23). As I mentioned above these are proto-vertical lines. By age two years and nine months, vertical direction is becoming clearer when Joel makes a series of longitudinal lines but this time using pushing lines (see Figure 24). He names each line, one at a time, as he draws them, saying, 'Mummy, Daddy, Joel and Ben'. The subject matter of the family group is typical of early drawings. Here Joel captures the vertical axis of the most important people he knows. Additionally, the concept of *parallelism* is being formed – long before he knows the term *parallel*. People may stand side by side; lines may travel in the same direction.

This is also the beginning of composition. Claire Golomb (1992) writes very interestingly about the different ways children compose their pictures and how these become integrated as they grow older. Nancy Smith (1983)

Figure 23   Joel, aged one year and six months, places lines side by side, leaving gaps between them. He makes the lines by pulling the pen towards his own body

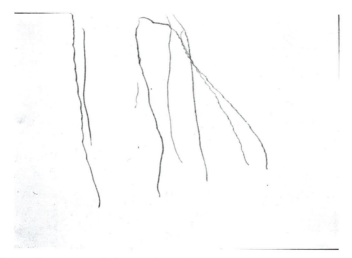

Figure 24   Joel, aged two years and nine months, makes a series of longitudinal lines by pushing the pen away from his body to make each line, saying as he does so, 'Mummy, Daddy, Joel and Ben'. He is representing the vertical axes of human figures. The concept of parallelism is also forming

and Pat Tarr (1990) have also written sensitively about the very young child's arrangements of marks on paper. Other researchers seem to regard composition and design as a sort of optional extra to the real concerns of showing space and shape. Yet, for many children, including the very young, it is clear that their organisation of shapes, colours, marks or objects is driven and guided by an aesthetic sense, involving feelings and intuitions about harmony, balance, composition and design. Many researchers behave as if these can be separated and neglected from the study of drawing. This is nonsensical of course, because composition is involved at every level in drawing skills. It is impossible to analyse how children draw the structure of objects and scenes without simultaneously considering their composition.

Composition involves a child's movements. Sometimes, Joel, like other children, not only separates each mark, but also each marking movement, by replacing and removing each pen cap between each stroke! At other times he puts his fingers into them. He seems to use them as finger-puppets, sometimes speaking to them or pretending they can speak. Chris Athey tells me that she has also noticed children playing with pen caps in this way. Like other movements, they are not an irrelevance but deeply important as drawing and painting develop. In play, Joel is temporarily released from the struggle of adapting his movements to solely the *functional* aspects of the pens. He has the freedom to handle them in very different ways and to find out all sorts of ways to use them. He has the opportunity to manipulate these objects in a patterned sequence of actions which has grace and style. The movements are also overlayed with expressive and emotional values. The pens and pen caps become identities, personalities even. So, talking to your pens affects your drawing!

Joel is very selective about where he puts his marks in space. In a small drawing book at this time, he starts a new page for each mark. This is important in terms of early writing and mathematical logic. It may also show Joel's understandings of objects in space (Smith, 1983; Athey, 1990; Matthews, 1999).

Points in space

Sometimes Joel makes layers of marks, sometimes he clusters them in tight groups, and at other times they are scattered across a wide area or else carefully restricted in one place. Each mark on the paper seems to be a unique event. Each new impact of the brush seems to be an attempt to repeat this unique event!

Continuous rotations

By the age of one year and eleven months, Ben's, Joel's and Hannah's push-pulls and arcs are becoming far more controlled and can be more or less expansive, as the child chooses. One important example is when, by adapting the movements of the wrist, elbow and shoulder, these back-and-forth and side-to-side, fanning, thrusting and dragging movements are 'opened-up', as it were, to become *continuous rotations*. See Figure 25, drawn in spilt milk by Hannah aged two years and seven months.

Figure 25   Hannah, aged two years and seven months, makes a continuous rotation in spilt milk on a vinyl surface

Figure 25a   Robert, aged three years and one month, draws a continuous rotation *in electronic paint with a mouse-driven personal computer*

Nancy Smith (1983) suggests that these continuous rotations enable a child to make a prolonged movement. This is hard to do with other sorts of movements. It was not possible with arcs and push-pulls. When children run along a long beach, they can make a very long, straight line, but usually the line has to stop rather abruptly because space runs out. In tracing an elliptical course, however, one can go on for as long as one wants. There is also present here the notion of repetition (Smith, 1983).

Children quickly learn to vary the speed of their continuous rotations and they use these accelerations and decelerations for expressive effects. This means that they change the speed of the rotation according to feelings and emotions.

So powerful are these strategies for establishing a relationship between the actions of the child and their effects, that they are transported from one medium or context to another. John Jessel and I discovered that very young children used horizontal arc, vertical arc, push pull and continuous rotation when they encountered, for the first time, electronic paint.

Traditional drawing media and electronic paint

Changing the medium causes variations in children's drawing actions. John Jessel and I introduced children, between the ages of one year and ten months and three years and ten months, to the microcomputer paintbox (Matthews and Jessel, 1993a; 1993b). We compared the drawings they produced in traditional media (pencils, coloured felt-tip pens or crayons and paper) with those produced in 'electronic paint'. This medium differs from traditional painting and drawing media in important ways. The drawing surface and the display surface are separated and are at right angles to each other. Electronic paint has no physical texture and colour does not 'run out' or mix on the surface. Nor is there any loss of luminosity. Sometimes the screen displays only a small part of one's drawing action and we observed Robert (aged three years and one month) slowing his drawing movements in order to be sure that this was the case.

Yet even with these differences we found that children used horizontal arcs and push-pulls to make links between their movements and the visual effects. More complex shapes, like continuous rotations (see Figure 25a), grids and closures were also produced in electronic paint. We found that one drawing movement, the vertical arc, was radically modified because, with the mouse-driven computer, movements made in the third dimension (waving the mouse in the air, or banging it on the table) does not produce effects on the screen – at least – not directly.

Covering and hiding

When children begin to make large rotations, at the same time they love to 'cover' an area of paper. Of course, it is relatively straightforward to do this with paint and a large brush. Ben covers an A2 sheet of paper with red and pink paint and says it is, 'Toast and jam with Gypsy'. Gypsy was a friend of his. The surface of the paper represented the surface of the toast, and the spreading of the paint represented the spreading of the jam. In this case, rotational or other movements are sufficient to cause surfaces to be actually, physically, covered with paint. Sometimes, when armed only with a pencil or a felt-tip pen, the intention still seems to be to 'cover' an area, but, of course, it is more difficult when using a fine-tipped drawing instrument. Paint allows areas to be completely covered, but when one uses a pencil or similar tool, gaps are left. In such instances, speed is of the essence, and the spare and open weave of lines is understood by the child to mean completely in-filled areas. One has to therefore 'pretend' that these holes do not exist and that one intends that the open weave of lines 'stands for' the act of covering or concealing. The related device of 'crossing out' is a later, conventionalised development of these covering strategies formed in infancy. As we will see, many sophisticated, mathematical or linguistic signs have their roots in actions performed by the infant on the world.

This phenomenon also contradicts the traditional assumption that only much later on in childhood do children use a continuous, all-embracing line to stand for an object. Before the age of two, children are developing, in their so-called 'scribbling', something akin to what we might term 'sketching'. The idea that 'sketching' does not appear until children are much older (Fenson, 1985; Cox, 1992) needs to be looked at again. It seems likely that the beginnings of sketching can be glimpsed in the continuous rotational marks made by young children. Later we shall see how Joel develops early sketching techniques.

Many accounts of children's drawing stress the process through which children select (from so-called 'scribbling') clear shapes like circles and lines which they combine to make designs and pictures (for example, Kellogg, 1969). However, this is only part of the story. The child also explores the continuous-contact line (misnamed by adults as 'scribble'). These two interrelated processes – the making of clearly defined shapes and the continuous-contact line – entwine together and enrich each other. Together, they help the child become fluent in drawing.

Closed shape

Usually, it is through using rotational movements that children discover how to make a closed shape. This is extremely important in drawing development. As Arnheim (1954, 1974) writes, space is never neutral. The closed shape creates two very different regions separated by a line. It separates a portion of space from the surrounding area. Very young children quickly learn to use it to show a *face* of an object and/or its *volume*. They also find that with the closed shape they represent inside and outside relationships. This interest may reflect the child's changing understanding of space and volume. Children modify their understanding that two objects cannot occupy one space. Earlier in infancy, in their investigation of shape, location and movement, infants discover that one object cannot occupy the space of another object (Bower, 1974, 1982). Now, with the discovery that one object can go inside a container of some kind, they modify this understanding. They begin to draw one two-dimensional object (a mark or shape) inside another two-dimensional object, a closed shape. See Figure 26, by Hannah, aged two years and five months. This inside–outside relationship quickly attracts other levels of meaning. Inside and outside relationships appearing upon the drawing

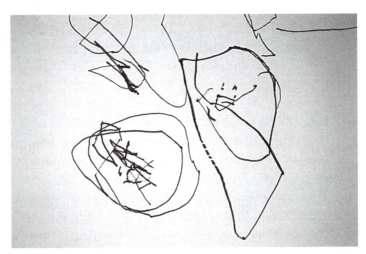

Figure 26   Rotational drawing sometimes results in closed shapes. *Hannah, aged two years and five months, draws closed shapes and places marks inside them*

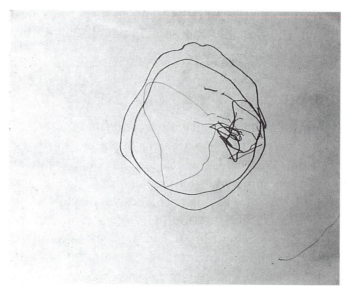

Figure 27 Joel, aged two years and five months, draws a closed shape into which he makes a little squiggle. He says (about the squiggle inside the closed shape), 'There's a baby in here. A baby in the water'

surface come to represent inside–outside relationships in real or imagined world (Athey, 1990; Matthews, 1984; 1994; 1999). A powerful example is when Joel, not quite two and a half, draws a little mark inside a closed shape. He explains the drawing by saying, 'There's a baby in here ... A baby in the water'. (See Figure 27.)

In some drawings children place the marks anywhere inside the closure. However, in other drawings, children are careful about which part of the interior the marks are placed. Sometimes children will place different *types* of mark in different *locations* inside closed shapes. For instance, Joel, at two years and two months, places a group of roughly parallel lines to the right side of the interior of a closure, and a rotational mark to the left side of the interior (see Figure 28). By grouping marks according to type, he is beginning a process of classification. This is the start of mathematical logic.

The use of the closed shape as a representation of inside and outside relations only occurs if the child is already developing these ideas. Just being able to make the shapes in a motoric sense, does not necessarily mean that symbolic or representational meanings are attached to them – a subtle but crucial distinction when one interprets children's drawing. Usually, however, the development of skilled, self-directed actions coincides with development of the ideas – they quickly become one and the same. When children begin to use the closed shape in their drawings, this means that there has been an important shift in the development of both motor-control and thinking.

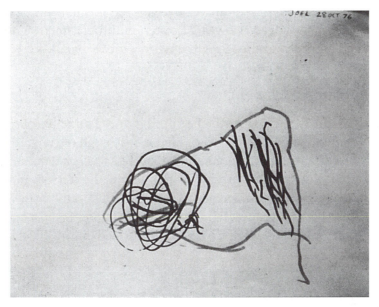

Figure 28   Joel, aged two years and two months, sorts out different types of marks by placing them in distinctly different locations within a closed shape; rotational lines to the left, parallel lines to the right

Putting shapes together, taking them apart and putting them together again

The closed shape is one of a family of shapes which are created. Rudolf Arnheim (1954, 1974) suggests that the child learns, not only to put actions and shapes together, but also to take them apart. For example, Hannah, at the age of sixteen months, separates a pulling action from pushing action. She draws a roughly vertical, roughly parallel series of lines, by repeatedly pulling the pen over the edge of a piece of paper. Similarly, at around age two, horizontal arcs are deconstructed into roughly horizontal lines (see Figure 29). However, we must be cautious about calling such lines 'vertical' or 'horizontal' since, strictly speaking, these are really the result of actions made to and from the body, and latter are made from side-to-side movements across the midline of the chest. We should really consider the emergent vertical line as a *longitudinal* and the emergent horizontal as *lateral*. Later they will be used to define vertical and horizontal directions. A good example is Figure 24, in which Joel, at two years and nine months makes a series of pushing, or lon-gitudinal lines, calling them 'Mummy, Daddy, Joel and Ben'. The child grad-ually defines upon the drawing surface two main co-ordinates, which we may think of as X and Y co-ordinates. We can see this happening in Figure 30, a drawing by Ben, aged two years and ten months. Lateral ('horizontal') parallels are contrasted against longitudinal ('vertical') parallels.

Right-angular attachment

In Figures 29 and 30 we also see the beginnings of the principle of *right-angu-lar attachment*, in which X and Y co-ordinates are joined (Figures 29 and 30). This very important visual structure is discovered when lateral movements (derived from horizontal arcs) are combined with vertical movements derived from longitudinal movements – movement to and from the body. Lines may also be attached to each other at right angles. Later, a co-ordinate system of horizontals and vertical axes will be formed on the drawing surface (see Figure 30).

Making connections: joining things together

Children begin to use a line to join two separate marks or patches together. They think about whether things are continuous or separated and how some things are linked together. Their play helps guide their drawing and their understanding of these relationships in the real world. In this way, the draw-ing surface becomes an 'analogue space' (Wolf, 1983, personal communica-tion) for the real world and a workspace for sorting out conscious and unconscious thought.

Combining movements and marks: travelling zigzags, waves and travelling loops

At around two years of age Ben, Joel and Hannah are all able to separate out, or combine, the different parts of movements and shapes. They can use a continuous line to enclose other shapes; they can place marks inside or out-side closed shapes and they can join lines to each other. They can group lines and marks in ways which are logicomathematical, rhythmical, spatial and musical. They can put together movements which were initially separate to make more complex movements. In this way new shapes are created.

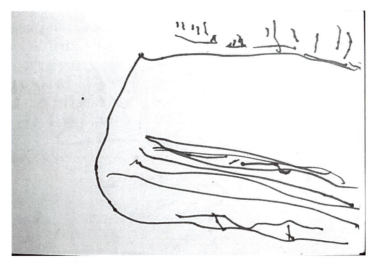

Figure 29 Right-angular attachment, *plus* lateral *and* longitudinal seriation *of lines. The concept of* parallelism *is also forming. A drawing by Ben, aged two years and ten months*

Figure 30 Right-angular attachment *is formed when lateral lines are combined with longitudinal lines. A drawing by Ben, aged three years and three months. As directional changes are mastered, so he can make other sorts of lines, like a* travelling zigzag *(at the right of the drawing)*

Travelling zigzags and travelling waves

Between the ages of twenty-three and twenty-six months both Hannah and Ben combined a push-pull movement with a sideways movement of the drawing hand to produce a *travelling zigzag* (see Figures 30, 31 and 32). In Figure 31, Hannah, aged three years and three months, makes a *travelling zigzag* or *wave* while saying, 'The clouds are moving along slowly'. A few days later she combines travelling zigzags with horizontal arcs and vertical arcs which produce dots or points. As she draws, she says, 'the clouds are moving along and the rain is coming down'. She is showing two different aspects of falling rain; as sheets of water pouring through a vertical axis (*travelling zigzags*), and as individual droplets hitting the ground (dots produced by *vertical arc* at bottom right). (See Figure 32).

Figure 31   Hannah, aged three years and three months, makes travelling zigzags

Figure 32   Hannah, aged three years and three months, soon combines travelling zigzags *or* travelling waves *with* horizontal arcs *(middle of drawing) and* vertical arcs *which produce dots or points (bottom right)*

Travelling loops

A travelling loop is created by a push-pull which crosses back over itself between pull and push, producing successions of 'e' shapes of various kinds. Other wave-like and spiralling shapes are discovered in this way. In Figure 33, Hannah, aged three years and two months, makes a travelling loop while saying, 'The bubbles are going up to the surface'. The line does not only spiral, it spirals through a vertical axis along which higher and lower relationships are established. The representation of ascent and descent is practised in play. One important example is when handheld toys are flown up and down. In many observations I made, children also create ascending or descending spirals with handheld toys, combining elliptical orbits with rising and falling. This trajectory in three-dimensions, plus the dimension of time, is mapped onto the two-dimensional drawing surface.

Figure 33   Hannah, aged three years and two months, makes a travelling loop. *'The bubbles are going up to the surface' she says*

Different movements have different results

Children explore the relationship between their movements in different contexts and in different media over and over again. Hannah, aged two years and seven months, sits at the kitchen table which is covered with a vinyl sheet. She splashes milk from her cup onto the table and this forms striking patterns as it spreads across the shiny surface. She studies the white shapes intently and practises, in sequence, distinctly different marking actions. First, looking very closely at what she is doing, she trails a line through the milk using one finger, then she trails four fingers through it. She attends very closely to the effects of her actions. She is seeing that different movements have different results.

The same movements but in different media

Children discover that the same type of action can be practised in a variety of settings and media. The actions are modified in relation to the possibilities and constraints of the medium. For example, different kinds of rotations may be produced with the palm of the hand in milk (Figure 25) or with mouse-driven electronic paint (Figure 25a).

Combining different drawing actions

Hannah can make a variety of straight lines and circular shapes. She has become an expert at producing these and other shapes. From two years and one month Hannah's rotational shape is quite accomplished. She can combine or separate marks and marking actions at will. She can play around with variations of speed and intensity. She can choose to spiral inwards or outwards according to whim. She can slow down and curtail the rotational movement to create near single-line enclosures. In this way she can produce a shape which we have seen is very important to drawing development: the closed shape. Or she can attach the lines to the closed shape to make another very important visual form: the *core and radial* (Figure 34) (Athey, 1990). Joel and Ben were also able to produce these shapes at around the same age. The core and radial structure is really a special case of right-angular attachment.

Figure 34   Hannah, aged two years and six months, makes a core and radial

U shape on baseline

Another development of right-angular attachment is when a line is made to depart from a baseline at approximate right angles and then is made to return to that baseline, forming another kind of closure. I call this a U shape on baseline (see Figure 35). It is a useful discovery for the child, because the principle can be used to generate a variety of structures. For example, U shapes may be attached to other U shapes to form multi-cellular structures.

Children need to practise and repeat what they know

These discoveries are not made once and for all. What is discovered on one occasion may not necessarily be remembered. The same discoveries might need to be made many times and in many contexts, so that these understandings overlap, as it were, forming powerful concepts. Even when shapes are put together it might be necessary for the child to repeatedly take them apart again in order to really establish how the different parts relate together, and how movements and shape relate to each other. The child does not necessarily abandon earlier forms of drawing action in favour of later ones. As we saw, Hannah investigated and reinvestigated the same things over and over again,

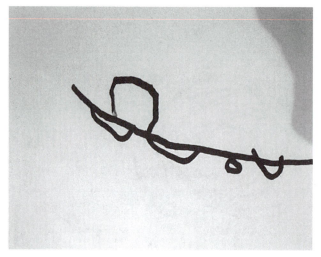

Figure 35 Ben, aged three years and two months, forms U Shape on baseline. *This is a development of right-angular attachment*

and will continue to do so, in different contexts and in different media.

However, each new experience is not simply a repetition. Each new version adds some new quality or understanding to the shapes and movements which produced them; subtle or radical permutations and overlays of emotion. It may be true, as Claire Golomb (1992) writes, that prior scribbling experience is not necessary for the child to draw certain shapes, for example, the closed shape. However, it is likely that these shapes will remain primitive without practice. Without practice, children seem unable to put shapes together in new ways. Through practice, both the basic shapes and the structural principles which produced them, become enriched by new possibilities.

Between the ages of two and a half and three years and two months, Ben, Joel and Hannah are all well on the way to producing a variety of lines and shapes. They make *continuous rotations*, closed-shapes, parallel lines, right-angular connections, travelling zigzags (see Figures 36–40). Sometimes all these are combined within a single drawing (see Figure 36).

When lines are intentionally coincided, or when a sequence of dots follows the path of a preceding line, I call this *collinearity* or *shared pathways*. You can see a little of this in Figure 36 and also in Figure 38.

The shapes are practised for their own sake but may also have representational values. In Figure 40, for example, Ben uses roughly parallel lines and near right-angular structure within a closed shape to show a man fighting snakes in a snake pit.

A development of *core and radial* is the *tadpole figure*. Figures 49 and 50 are good examples.

Figure 36 A drawing by Hannah, aged two years and six months, combines continuous rotations, closed-shapes, parallel lines, right-angular connections *and travelling zigzags. She also marks beginnings and ends of lines*

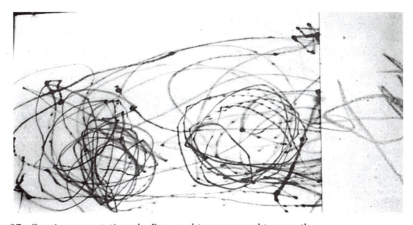

Figure 37 Continuous rotations *by Ben, aged two years and ten months*

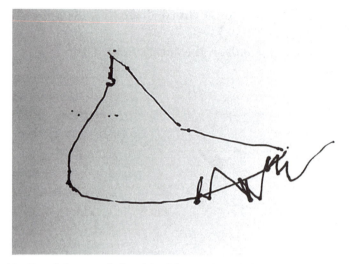

Figure 38 Closed shape *made from joined lines and* travelling zigzag. *In making the zigzag, Ben has tried to follow the bottom line of the closed shape. I call this* collinearity *or* shared pathways. *A drawing by Ben, aged three years and one month*

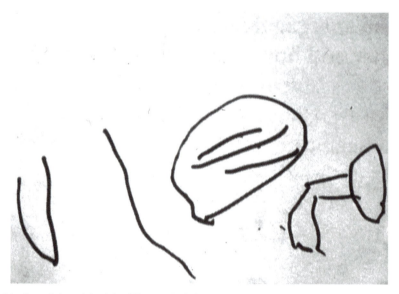

Figure 39 From left to right: joined line; a single longitudinal line; closed shape with parallel lines inside and tadpole figure (note the jointed legs and feet), by Ben, aged three years and two months

Going around, going up, going down and going through

Children discover ways of representing inside, outside, things that touch, connect or are attached and things which cover other things.

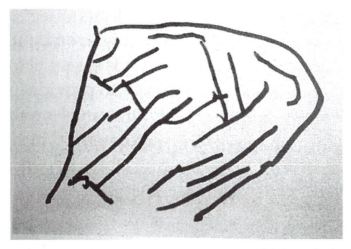

Figure 40　Parallel lines and right-angle connections represent a man fighting snakes in a snake pit, by Ben, aged three years and two months

In a certain, concrete sense, they can represent things which are close to each other, things which are far away from each other and things which go along in the same direction. The surface of the paper serves as an actual, physical plane onto which all of these, and other, relationships and movements (including touchingness, connectivity, going over, going under, going in, going out) can be mapped in a direct, physical sense. For example, a line or mark passing between two parallel lines can be said to 'go through'.

The possibility of representing physical ascent and descent may also be realised when the drawing surface is vertical or sloping, for example, on an easel. All these relations may be actually, physically enacted on the physical plane of the paper or other drawing surface.

But there are other senses in which going up, going down and going through (along with other relationships and other directions of travel) require that the plane of the drawing surface refer to a space other than its actual, physical surface. These include, 'higher and lower' relationships, in the sense of moving through an *imaginary* vertical axis, and 'going through', in the sense of the passage along and through a bound volume and also in the sense of going away *imaginatively*, into the distance, back 'through' the picture plane. Again, these axes and relationships are discovered and investigated in play. They are based upon vectors of movement practised with the entire body through space, but especially in miniaturised, hypothetical worlds of pretend play with handheld objects.

Round and round, going up, going down and going through

Paradoxically, by using drawing to capture information about the object irrespective of viewpoint, children sometimes arrive at possible views of objects. These representational possibilities are practised and consolidated in play. We saw this happen with Joel, from the age of two years and eleven months. For example, he plays with toy-people and a coffee-grinder, moving the handheld figures around, up and over, and through the grinder. In England's mountainous Lake District, Joel plays with toy figures who are made to move around and around, up, over and down, large rocks, outside the caravan in which we are staying. He also has the experience of climbing, with his parents, up, down and around the craggy fells.

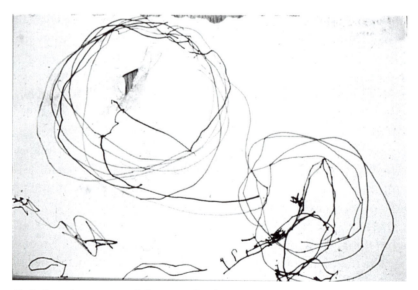

Figure 41   Joel, aged two years and eleven months, draws a mountain and climbers

Then, when he draws people climbing a mountain, he plays with ideas about three basic axes of movement; going around and around, going up, going down and going through. Figure 41 shows going around a mountain (upper left); going up, over and down a mountain (lower right). As a consequence of enacting the movement around and up, over and down the mountain, he arrives at two possible views of the object. Essentially by-products of action-representations, *side-elevation* and *plan* appear. These are called projective relationships. They show two different projections of the mountain. However, the other direction of travel, going through, though demonstrated in this drawing, is not represented as a projective relationship. He enacts going through the mountain by making a hole in the paper with his pen (upper left).

As I mentioned above, sometimes the paper does not refer to a space other than itself, but is what it is, a physical surface. It is an object, a physical plane, which is used as a prop to emulate spatial movements. 'Going through', is one such direction of movement which is initially demonstrated in this way.

At this age, the only way Joel can manage this third dimension is by actually poking the pencil through the paper (Matthews, 1984). Very young children often investigate 'going through' by poking holes in their paintings and drawings. Here is an example from observations made of Hannah at the age of three years and five months:

Hannah makes a pencil drawing. The movement of the pencil-point becomes the movement of the 'dancer'. She pushes the pencil right through the paper, saying as she does so, 'I danced through the hole and fell through. It has a hole in the other side ...'. She considers for a moment her last statement and then says, bursting with laughter, 'It has to have!'

Children at this time are often interested in many different examples of 'going through'. They like crawling or sliding through tubes; they like pouring sand or liquid through tubes. They also like looking through tubes; cardboard tubes, telescopes, cameras and any number of items which have holes, meshes, or grids through which can pass light. Drawings and paintings become perforated and used as masks. 'Peepo' games, initiated as we have seen, much earlier in babyhood with a caregiver, have now undergone transformation. Picture-books which use cut-outs in the pages, so that you can see through to the next page, are very popular. The Ahlbergs' book is a good example. It takes its title from the 'Peepo' game (Ahlberg and Ahlberg, 1981). Children start to understand about lines of sight and points of view from these investigations and when they play hiding games. A teacher can build upon this understanding in a number of ways.

Such understandings of viewpoint are also the basis of later understanding of projective relationships in drawings, that is, drawings which show depth. One such projective system is linear perspective. The basis of linear perspective is closing one eye, standing still and looking at the scene through one eye. In an observation I made in a Singaporean kindergarten, Chinese four-year-olds manipulate toy spacecraft, causing them to whirl up and down and in circles in space and time. On occasions, one girl holds her toy spacecraft before her face, looking at it with one eye, while placing the palm of her other hand over her other eye. She is obtaining a single, or monocular, image of the object from her position relative to it. She can maintain the same viewpoint relative to the object whether she spins on her own axis, or slows the spacecraft to a standstill in space (Matthews, 1999). Obtaining a monocular or one-eyed view of an object forms the basis of an important observational drawing tradition originating from Europe (see Figure 118 in Chapter 8). Yet this four-year-old has not copied this from anyone, nor has she learned it in an 'art-lesson'. She has discovered it from play, because, in order to fulfil the requirements of her visual and dynamic narrative, she needs to incorporate some single images of the shape. She is building up understandings of projective geometry and how one might obtain a single, monocular, image of the things and scenes.

It is this concept which, in a study I am making, in Singapore, with Rebecca Chan, enables young children as young as two years of age to use a video camera and make movies. The children adapt concepts emerging in playful and explorative activities, including drawing, to help them use the camera. For example, concepts of line of sight and going through are adapted for use of the viewfinder or viewing screen of the camera, so that the children can point the camera and select shots (Ma Ying and Leong, 2002; Chan and Matthews, 2002b). Some of you might object, 'but surely the children don't understand what is happening when they use the camera?' The first answer to that is another question: 'Do you?'

My studies of young children's use of computer paintbox and electronic lens media, show that children use the same investigative and expressive movements and emergent concepts across different media. The concepts and actions are adapted according to the different possibilities. This means that the drawing movements I have discussed in this chapter are generalised categories. Because people cannot 'see' what children's early drawings are 'about', it is presumed that there is no content at all. But there is, and it is essential to know how to recognise what drawings are about if we are to provide for and nurture the development of representational thinking and the use of symbols and signs. Early drawings are about shapes; the shapes on the paper and the shapes of the movements which produce them and their relationship to objects and events in the world.

Summary

We have seen that children progress from initial exploratory mark-making to powerful marking strategies which partially reflect the natural movements of the body. However, it would be a mistake to think of these actions as just thoughtless, mechanical movements. Children's drawing actions are sensitive to fluctuations in mood, both their own and those of people around. We noted that recent research suggests that all forms of symbolisation and representation, including speech and drawing, may be based upon babies' body actions which are articulated into a kind of dynamic language (Allott, 2001).

As the child matures, these actions and shapes are further differentiated and sorted into groups. This is not merely a gradual assembling of a vocabulary of shapes to be used later, in the making of designs or pictures, in the way that Kellogg and others describe. Rather, throughout this process, the child imbues drawing actions, and the shapes these make, with emotion and representational possibilities. They are interested in beginnings and ends of lines, and map these onto the drawing surface. They attach lines to each other at angles. They colour-code their actions. They also experiment with covering one layer of paint over another. On the drawing surface, the child represents, inside and outside relationships, as well as basic directions of movement, across, round and round, and up and down. Language is involved in this process. They talk about what they are doing and associate the appropriate words with shapes and their relationships. This assists language acquisition, but in turn, language helps guide and organise drawing. These shapes, relationships and directions of movement serve as the co-ordinates for later drawing. Additionally, we can discern in the investigations representational play and, in the drawing of the very young, the beginnings of representation of viewpoint.

We have seen how children develop some powerful drawing rules. In the next chapter we will see how children use these rules to make new combinations of shapes. They become interested in colour and shape relationships in themselves, but they also use the effects these have to work out new ideas about their experience and the world. It seems as if they realise that relationships emerging on the drawing surface are, in some respects, like relationships in the real world. They start to co-ordinate a family of relationships in such a way that they build up descriptions of reality. It is crucial to note that this is in no way a copy of reality, but the child discovering, using and being guided by the internal logic and systematicity of the representational process. Additionally, my recent studies of early representation show that actions and concepts developed in drawing are carried across into children's introduction to electronic and information technology (IT) media.

5

Seeing and knowing

As children grow older, they seem to want to capture, in their drawings, more information about the shapes and structures of objects which interest them. In doing this, they sometimes produce drawings which turn out odd-looking to some adults. This is because the drawings do not always show a possible view of an object. (See Figures 42, 43, 44 and 45.) Figure 42 (by Campbell, an Australian Singaporean aged four years and seven months) shows people sitting around a table. Why is the table drawn like this, as an approximate rectangle, with the figures grouped around top and bottom edges, making one figure 'upside-down', so to speak, from a viewer's point of view? Figure 43 shows another drawing of people at a table. This drawing may be a little further along a developmental trail, since the figures are now aligned along a vertical axis. But why is the table drawn like this, with the legs spread out? Surely the intention is not to show a badly made, collapsed table? Figure 44 also shows people around a table, yet it is drawn in a quite different way. What exactly determines the difference? What about Figure 45, with the horses apparently doing the four-legged splits? Is this a collapsed horse, a bit like a collapsed table? What are the children trying to do?

There have been at least 100 years of discussion about why children produce drawings like this. One classic theory, which continues to influence psychologists and educators today, is the idea that children move through a stage of *intellectual realism*, in which they try to capture their idea of the object's true shapes, regardless of viewpoint, to *visual realism*, when they capture a view of the object as if seen from a single position.

This theory derives from a combination of the work of two men, Jean Piaget and Georges Luquet. The original ideas of these men were very complex, but their theories have since been watered down by other people. The simplified version of the theory of intellectual and visual realism, argues that

Figure 42 An Australian Singaporean child, Campbell, aged four years and seven months, draws people sitting around a table upon which rest objects

Figure 43 A six-year-old Londoner's drawing of people standing near a table upon which rest objects

children below seven years of age draw what they 'know' and that only in later childhood can they draw what they 'see'. Hence, according to this approach, Figures 42 and 43 show the child trying to capture the true shapes and major axes of the scene – table, people and other objects – irrespective of any possible view of the overall scene. Figure 44, on the other hand, shows

Figure 44   A seven-year-old Chinese Singaporean child's drawing of people sitting at a table upon which rest objects

Figure 45   A six-year-old Londoner's drawing of horses in a field

similar subject matter – people around a table – but in this case the child has not captured the true, rectangular shape of the table top but has distorted the shape of the table-top to show a possible view of the table and the people around it. In Figures 42 and 43, the body-parts (faces, bodies, legs, arms, hands and so on) are shown clearly and in sequence, but as simple shapes, conveying volumes (which may be roughly spherical [heads] or elongated [bodies]; slab-like [palms of hands]), with stick-like forms attached (fingers, hair) (Willats, 1997).

In contrast, the people around the table in Figure 44, though also reduced to fairly simple shapes, denote more than undifferentiated lumps, slabs and rods, but are designed so as to allude to curving volumes in a three-dimensional space (Willats, 1997; Tormey and Whale, 2002; Whale, 2002). They are drawn as notional side views, front views and back views.

Again, in Figure 42, every form is drawn with an uninterrupted boundary. (There is, in this drawing, one important exception, to which I will return shortly.) Forms also remain entire in Figure 43, except that this time they are superimposed over each other. In contrast, in Figure 44, contour lines of a form may be broken, where another form, imagined to be closer to the viewer of the picture, partially hides this further form. According to the classical theory, with maturation, the child moves from the former stage of intellectual realism (arguably exemplified in Figures 42 and 43) to the latter stage of visual realism (arguably exemplified in Figure 44).

The theory would explain Figure 45 in terms of the child moving from the former to the latter stage in her different versions of the horse. The child seems to be asking herself, 'just how *do* you draw horses in a field?' She has tried every way she can think of. In the first image, the one in which the horse seems spreadeagled on the ground, the child seems to be reconstructing the horse as if it is a bit like a table, consisting as it does of a large region (its body) with a leg in each corner, attached at approximate right angles. However, in drawing a horse (or table) like this, although it captures some of the truth about the object (in itself, as Piaget put it), the result looks odd (Willats, 1997). The child's task is to reconcile information about the true shapes of the object and their relationship within an object, while at the same time showing a credible view of the object (Duthie, 1985). Some of this reconciliation may be evident in the image of the 'collapsed' horse, in which two of the legs are drawn as oblique lines rather than attached at rightangles. This might be a sort of compromise between drawing an intellectually realistic horse and a visually realistic horse. We can see the child struggling to work this out as she progresses through a series of variations of the horse, culminating in one in which she does not try to capture the horse's legs in their entirety, but shows a possible view of the horse, with the two legs most distant from the viewer, partially hidden (or occluded) by the two legs closer to the viewer.

Or at least, so the story goes. But is it true? Is this the best way to describe what children are doing? The idea of different modes of realism derives from the Georges Luquet's theory but was unfortunately appropriated by Piaget, who distorted the idea in the process. To be fair, both these men thought that the relationship between what we call 'seeing' and what we call 'knowing' was a very complex one, involving changing relationships between perception, cognition and representation. Nowadays, however, the conventional wisdom lumps together many different types of drawing under either category of intellectual or visual realism.

Although this idea still influences many people's understanding of drawing development, it is very unsatisfactory. One reason is that it is very difficult, if not impossible, to separate 'seeing' from 'knowing'. Nor is the reason children do not produce visually realistic pictures accounted for solely in terms of the child's supposed inability to capture views of the object (as Piaget thought). My own studies (Matthews, 1999; 2002 in press), and those of John Willats (1997) show that children are aware of views, and in some situations are able to draw these. In Figure 42, for example, can we not argue that the artist partially occludes, or hides, the lower parts of the human bodies, by the edge of the table?

This would simultaneously dispose of the claim that children cannot show view-specific information because they are simply unable to produce the kinds of shapes and line junctions necessary to show possible views of objects. Indeed, earlier work by Phillips, Hobbs and Pratt (1978) shows that children are able to form quite complex line junctions and shapes, when these are not tied to any commitment to representing a view of a real object. For example, when children were shown two-dimensional patterns which incorporated the line junctions necessary for producing a view of a cube, they were quite capable of copying these shapes.

Nor, in any case, do the categories make much sense when drawings are analysed more carefully. Many children do not appear to pass neatly from one stage to another, but move through a series of dynamic systems which each capture and combine information in ways which are not accounted for in terms of a major division between intellectual and visual realism.

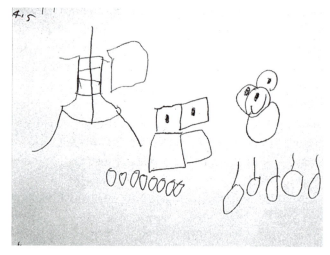

Figure 46   A three-year-old's drawing of a cube

It is unusual for very young children to choose to draw objects from observation in the sense of a 'still-life' practice. If we contrive situations in which
they are required to do so, then we need to be sensitive to their own ways of
drawing from observation. For a two- or three-year-old, it might not have
occurred to her that the drawing can be like a glimpse of an object as if seen
for one moment in time and from one position in space. My studies show
that children can indeed draw from observation, but the systems through
which they move have nothing to do with observational still-life practice as
is commonly understood in Western European art practice. If we look at the
drawings of even very young children, when they are asked to draw an object
we can see that the child tries to combine different sorts of information
deriving from different sensory channels and influenced by the child's language and concepts. When I asked two- and three-year-olds to draw a cube
with a ball resting on top of it, many of the three-year-old children were able
to draw acceptable squares and circles in order to describe the ball on top of
the cube. Of great significance however, is that, although the teachers were
quite happy with this solution, the children clearly were not. The children
persisted (sometimes in spite of persuasions to hurry up and finish their
drawings) with further versions of the cube. Many of these were unlike any
drawings of cubes I had ever seen before but were, nevertheless, intelligent
two-dimensional descriptions of cubes. Some these latter drawings show
each face of the cube as an approximate rectangle meeting at an edge (or at
vertex or corner), drawn as a line (Figure 46).

This means that the explanation for intellectually realistic drawings (so-called) is not accounted for by claiming that children are simply unable to draw views of objects – they can show views. However, they feel that by doing so, they might sacrifice some of the truth about the structure and characteristics of the object. So they form systems of representation little understood at present and which the classical theory of intellectual and visual realism nowhere near describes adequately. The child has the task of trying to keep the main characteristics of objects as well as how the object looks from a single viewpoint. Typically, children combine many sorts of information deriving from different perceptual channels, including touch and movement and also involving language and concepts.

Linda in dungarees

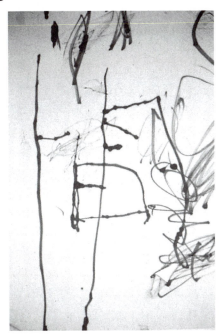

Figure 47 Ben, aged three years and two months, explores a two-dimensional structure for its own sake: parallel lines, right angles, closed shapes and wandering lines

Ben's drawing is such a case. Figures 47 and 48 show two works, drawn in the same red felt-tip pen which Ben has used for several days. Though both drawings are composed of similar shapes, lines and line junctions, they are different in other important respects. For instance, Figure 48 has representational values attributed to the lines whereas Figure 47 does not. In other words, one drawing (Figure 48) stands for something in the world, while the other draw-ing (Figure 47) does not stand for anything but is an exploration of lines and shapes for their own sake. Also, the way the pen is used differs between the two drawings, for example, in terms of applied pressure. It seems as though Ben's production of certain basic structures on the drawing surface has alerted him to the presence of these structures in the world. For several days now, Ben has joined lines at right angles, made parallel groups of lines, closed shapes and varieties of wandering lines (see Figure 47). Now that he is producing these forms and relationships on paper, he responds to and builds upon these emergent structures according to their internal logic, while, at the same time, noticing new examples of these structures within the environment.

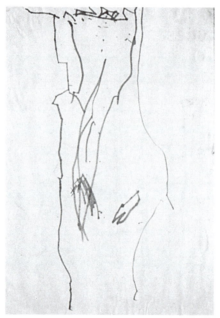

Figure 48 Ben, aged three years and two months, uses these structures to draw Linda in dungarees within the environment

One unusual example of parallel grouped lines is presented in the picture of his mother, Linda, standing near him, in the kitchen, wearing dungarees (see Figure 48).

Ben is aged three years and two months, and is sitting at the kitchen table using his favourite red felt-tip pen to draw a picture of Linda on a page of a small notepad. He does not represent her as a tadpole figure. In fact, this draw-ing precedes his first tadpole drawing. He looks back and forth between his drawing and her figure in order to produce this work. Some of the drawing can be accounted for in terms of the structural principles already described. The head or face is an angular closed-shape, squeezed in at the top of the drawing surface. Its small size in relation to the rest of the figure is not important to Ben. Just preserving the higher and lower relationship is what is important here. Some people would consider a drawing like this to be simply out of proportion. Such misinterpretations occur because adults do not understand children's priorities about the kind of information to be put into a drawing. This misunderstanding can be very destructive to a child. It is sometimes difficult for people to realise that their assumptions about 'correct' proportion arise from a particular theory about art and representation (Atkinson, 2002 forthcoming). Our responses to children arise directly from our interpretations of what they do, so it is crucial for teaching and childcare that we come to understand the assumptions which lie beneath these interpretations.

Ben may be using the angular closed shape to represent Linda's face, or perhaps the boundary of the volume of her head as a whole. Near the base of the drawing, this topological geometry is used to show the boundary of a hollow space. A pointed ellipse is used to denote Linda's bottom, perhaps meaning anus. He uses the powerful, perpendicular junction to create maximum differentiation or contrast between the arms and the body. Single strokes of the pen represent the entire tubular volumes of the arms. Similarly, single pen lines represent entire strips of denim – the straps of her dungarees.

However, it is the denotational values of the lines representing the boundaries of her body which are, perhaps, more surprising. In a controlled variation of movement along a vertical path, the line on the left actually specifies Linda's breast and waist, while the line at the right curves gently from the top of the drawing to form Linda's back, the small of her back, her behind and then the back of her thighs. So, he has represented the front and back of a female body. By doing this he has, in effect, also captured a view of her left side.

Observations of Ben drawing, plus the comments he made while drawing, suggest that he was representing the outermost boundaries of her body as they curved in and out, down the length of her body.

Different types of information

There are different ways this achievement might be interpreted. Such information may derive from a haptic, physical and sculptural knowledge of his mother's body, but it also suggests visual information deriving from his viewpoint; his line of sight to her from his position at the kitchen table.

A slightly different way of describing is to say that Ben draws what he 'knows' about the relationship of body parts to each other – what David Marr (1982) calls being 'object-centred', but in doing so arrives at a possible view of a human figure. This means the view of Linda, or the representation view-specific information, is a consequence – a by-product – of his drawing object-centred information. Or it may be that Ben quite consciously tries to find out how Linda will appear on paper from a given viewpoint. In looking at her and then drawing the contours of her body as they appear to him from his position at the kitchen table, 2 metres away, he captures her on paper from that viewpoint.

The two drawings by Ben (Figures 47 and 48) use the same shapes, and lines. However, the pressure on the pen is different in the drawing of Linda. This special variation in stress comes from his special interest in his mother. If he draws another object, or just draws just lines and shapes themselves, with no representational meaning, the variations of the line will be different.

When Ben changes the subject matter he changes the way he organises the shapes and lines he is familiar with to give them different meanings. In addition, he is capturing and combining different kinds of information and using them together so that he creates new representational meanings for lines. Although Ben turns out to be an unusually talented draughtsperson, this occurs with many children. Young children can show 'view-specific' information (as when Ben looks at and draws Linda from a particular viewpoint); or they can use 'object-centred' information, for example, when they draw the main features of something but not as seen from any particular viewpoint (Marr, 1982; Willats, 1997).

As the child produces a range of shapes and other visual structures, typically she will seek out those very shapes and structures from the visible environment. However, this does not mean that children's development in drawing is helped by an overemphasis on drawing directly from observation. Unfortunately, this has occurred in some areas of art education throughout the world. In British art education, some art advisers have failed to appreciate the importance of the approaches to drawing which children spontaneously generate. These people have tended to think of the drawings and paintings produced by children as limited and limiting stereotypes in which children are trapped and from which they should be rescued. Instead of nourishing and supporting a process akin to language acquisition, the beginnings of drawing have been undermined by a peculiarly limited version of a Western ethnocentric approach to visual representation. This, at its most destructive, is when all kinds of drawings, not made directly from nature, are prohibited. Another destructive approach is when the child is prematurely trained in techniques of supposedly famous and important artists. Sometimes, children's spontaneous art is devalued in contrast to the works of a 'great master'. Whether this exemplar be a great white male 'master' from Western art history, a famous Chinese painter, a contemporary Turner Prize winner or (just for a change) a female artist especially placed into the cultural spotlight, makes no difference. The child's own spontaneous visual representation and expression has been devalued in favour of a fixed, acceptable, cultural standard.

Nearly 100 years ago, Georges Luquet realised that children used different modes of representation, each being a powerful form of representation, of equal representational status with the others. This important insight has been lost today. Van Sommers (1984, p. 173), mistakenly writes of the 'tyranny' of children's drawing schemata which he feels 'retards' their development. Maureen Cox (1992; 1993; 1997; Cox, Cooke and Griffin, 1995), like many others, argues that before children can produce creative drawings they need to be purposely trained in representational skills. She argues that the kind of training she proposes is like correcting grammar and spelling. Ironically, by claiming this, she misses out a much more pertinent analogy between language acquisition and drawing development. Both processes are essentially creative in the sense that children generate language and drawing rules which change as they grow up (Chomsky, 1966; Willats, 1997). While early drawings, like first sentences, may seem strange, they are the result of powerful and intelligent hypotheses children make about language or drawing rules. It may be that the roots of all representational and symbolic systems occur in the basic body language of the infant, whether this is expressed in sounds, images or movements.

Having representational skills means becoming fluent with a range of techniques with different materials and different approaches to drawing. This entails much more than simply learning how to show perspective. Creativity means being able to detect and exploit symbolic and expressive opportunities in shapes, lines, and spaces on paper and in other forms. This creativity cannot be postponed while naïve perspective tricks are mastered. On the contrary, it is likely to be destroyed by such an approach.

Another psychologist, Ellen Winner (1989), writing about a highly prescriptive approach to drawing carried out in some Chinese schools, asks: 'How can Chinese children draw so well?' Comparing teaching in different cultures is fraught with difficulties. The problems have been compounded by stereotypes conjured up by any number of white anthropologists (amateur or professional) who suggest an incommensurable difference between the representation of different cultures. One oft cited but fallacious assumption is that Western artists' practice is about individual creativity, whereas Asian art is about conformity and apprenticeship into an accepted cultural form. While this false idea is happily accepted by those Asian dictators who want to rationalise and justify their oppression of their own citizens, it is not borne out in reality. My Chinese friends get rather irritated by this idea. They are just as creative and individualistic as Western artists, and by the same token, Western artists have also a long and ongoing apprenticeship system. Indeed, copying still occupies central stage in much Western contemporary art.

The evidence is that much – not all – of the precocious drawings that we see in China, Hong Kong, Singapore and elsewhere, and so much admired by tourist psychologists, have nothing whatsoever to do with the creative individualism of artists from Guo Xi to Ang Tee Tong, but are usually the product of highly repressive, prescriptive teaching methods. It is not a question of cultural or ethnic difference. Rigid, prescriptive practices, anywhere, impair children's ability to respond creatively and to initiate original ideas. This oppression takes many forms. London children might be forced to paint like Van Gogh, Singaporean children might have their drawings torn up in front of the class for not reproducing the teacher's exemplar. Whatever representational norm prevails, makes not a jot of difference. The real question to ask is not, 'how can Chinese children draw so well?' but, 'why is it that so many people think that this kind of drawing is good drawing?'

A few enlightened people, in early childhood education, and in art education, realise the significance of drawings like the one of Linda in dungarees (Figure 48). However, most people do not greet such drawings with the 'oohs' and 'aahhs' that are accorded the force-fed, hot-house picture-making of the world. Yet, Ben's drawing of Linda, and the ones which, in the next few days, followed, nevertheless capture information about how things look and how things are. Such information is essential in children's emergent literacy and representation.

Spilling milk while holding beans on toast: what things are, where things are and how and where they go

In this drawing, Ben, aged three years and two months, depicts himself as a tadpole figure, yet it comes later than the drawing of Linda in dungarees. The tadpole form is perfectly sufficient for this drawing which is about himself

Figure 49 Ben, aged three years and two months, holds a slice of beans on toast but drops a glass of milk

Figure 50 'A man digging in the ground for the bones of animals', by Ben, aged three years and three months

trying to hold a slice of beans on toast in one hand while carrying a glass of milk in the other (see Figure 49). In real life, it turns out to be very difficult to co-ordinate these two tasks (holding the slice of toast horizontally so that the beans do not slide off, while holding the glass of milk upright so that the milk does not spill). In Figure 49, he represents the moment in which he drops the glass of milk and it falls downwards through space accompanied by droplets of milk.

Since children during this phase are interested in how things connect, it follows that they are interested in the opposite of this – how things become disconnected or fall apart. Where things are, what things are, where they are at any given moment, and how and where they go, remain important concerns throughout life.

Now consider how all this information is conveyed on the drawing surface. Ben has realised the potential of closed-shapes to represent face-on views of faces (faces of people and faces of other objects too) and the potential of single lines to represent foreshortened planes. Perhaps he arrives at a foreshortened view of the beans on toast as a result of trying to show that the beans are 'on top of' the toast. Other shapes, for example, a square with dots inside it, may not have conveyed this information, suggesting that, rather than being 'on-top-of' the toast, the beans were 'inside' it. This would be another case of a viewer-centred drawing being the by-product of an object-centred drawing, and in this and other cases, language is involved.

We glimpsed beginnings of this ability to rotate events and objects through 90 degrees in drawings made at an earlier age. For example, in a drawing by Hannah, she shows the rain coming down as sheets of water through a vertical plane, and individual drops colliding with the ground at right angles. It might be the ability of children to imagine directions of movement which makes possible a later understanding of directions of view. These imaginative constructions of movement are assisted by freeplay with their bodies through space in addition to the miniaturised worlds invented in play with handheld objects moving through space.

From the age of one, in their play, Hannah, Ben and Joel enjoyed all kinds of twirlings and spinnings. You will remember the example of Hannah's continuous rotations. My research with South-East Asian children also shows them moving their whole bodies or handheld objects to represent the trajectories of objects in imaginary worlds, moving around and around, and up and down. These understandings are soon mapped onto the drawing surface.

Drawings like the one shown in Figure 49 contradict Piaget's verdict that children under the age of four show 'a complete lack of understanding of any sort of pictorial perspective' (Piaget and Inhelder, 1956, p. 173). His experiments showed children failing to represent foreshortened disks as single lines, and foreshortened sticks as dots, but persisting in representing these things as circles or lines respectively. He concluded that children had no conscious appreciation of their own viewpoint.

However, more recent research by John Willats has suggested that the problems which beset children when they draw foreshortened sticks and disks do not derive from a failure to understand viewpoint, but from the particular constraints presented by drawing (Willats, 1992; 1997). My own, informal experiments with Chinese Singaporean children drawing a straw hat with a brim, suggests that very young children are quite capable of recognising that a disk (in this case, the brim of the hat) may be represented as a single line, if the disk is seen totally foreshortened. When the hat is held in front of them with the brim totally foreshortened at their eye-level, many of the children started off their drawing with a single, horizontal line, clearly intending this to represent the foreshortened brim. However, they appear unhappy with this solution. What happens next is that they rethink and redraw the hat. Perhaps, although they can perfectly see that a disk looks like a line when seen edge-on, when it is drawn in this way, it no longer looks like a brim! A line does not communicate the disc-like structure of the object. The child has the problem of reconciling different types of information; that about the structural relationship within the objects and the relationship between the object and the viewer.

In drawing, the child has realised the potential of the closure to represent a face-on view of an object (in this case, a human 'face') and the potential of a line to specify an 'edge-on' or totally foreshortened view of the object. The moments-of-turn in between these two viewpoints are, of course, more difficult to master. This is because the object gradually appears to distort as it is turned through 90 degrees. To map this onto the drawing surface means changing the meanings of the use of line and shape. However, it is not long before the child is building up this kind of experience and will find ways to represent this idea, by transforming the drawing rules which allow the transformation of shape to show depth (Willats, 1997).

Children gain important ideas about moment-of-turn, or angular variation, through play. One example is when they play with opening and closing doors. Both my children (Londoners) and Singaporean Chinese, Malay and Indian children have been observed doing this (Matthews, 1999). Sometimes the way they vary the moment-of-turn in their pretend play with toys signifies important events. At other times, Joel and Hannah pretended that they themselves were doors, opening and closing, by slowly turning on the spot with arms outstretched. Sometimes adults were not allowed to pass by them without 'opening them', perhaps by pressing an imaginary switch.

Views, sections and surfaces

Children draw houses or people on a line representing the ground in ways which suggest, at least, the beginning of projective representation, or a kind of perspective. Figure 51 shows journeys by car and rail and is drawn mainly in a dynamic, topological gemeotry, capturing the continuity of passages of movement. However, by representing cars or trains by attaching U shapes to the baseline, Ben (aged three years and three months) is starting to represent objects resting on totally foreshortened planes. In Figure 51 Ben shows 'cars on a road'. In another (Figure 52) he shows a table with objects on it, showing an edge-on or foreshortened view of a table. This is clearly a development of the thinking involved in his drawing of beans resting on top of toast.

Figure 51 'Cars on a road', by Ben, aged three years and three months

Figure 52 'Objects on a table', by Ben, aged three years and three months

Figure 53 'Father Christmas on his sleigh with reindeer', by Ben, aged three years and three months. Letter shapes spell 'B-e-n' and are contained within the closed shape

There are other possibilities too. Look at Figure 50 which shows 'A man digging in the ground for the bones of animals'. Does the line of the ground show a section through the ground? Or is he using this line to show 'under' the ground? He showed the on-top-of relation by placing beans on the line representing the toast. As in the 'beans on toast' drawing, he is arriving at a representation of a foreshortened plane. This ground line is a view which he has to imagine – a sectional view. Ben is therefore doing more than showing 'on top' and 'underneath' relationships. My interpretation is supported by evidence from other drawings he made, in which he captures distinctly different, but equally true, features of objects. For example, in Figure 53 he has drawn the prong-like aspect of reindeers' antlers, whereas in Figure 54 he shows the gracefully curving shapes of the antlers as they might appear from a completely foreshortened view.

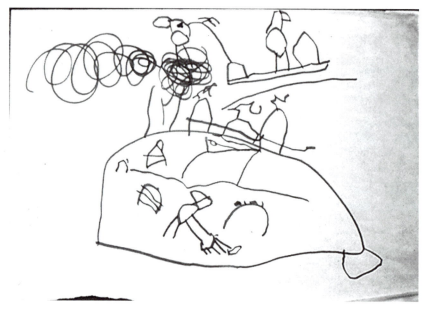

Figure 54 Father Christmas moves through two positions in time and space, from his sleigh to the chimney which he is about to descend, by going through, from outside the house to the inside. Ben is shown in bed; wrapped Christmas presents rest on a tabletop, while his mother, Linda, vacuum-cleans the floor

Young children often try to show several things at once. For example, when they draw hands they show them to be either prong-like or slab-like, or they combine both these characteristics (Willats, 1992; 1997).

Summary

In this chapter we have seen how children capture different types of information in their drawings. One type of information contained in their drawings concerns the main characteristics of objects irrespective of any fixed viewpoint. Another type of information is the shape of the object as seen from a particular viewpoint. Children combine these and other kinds of knowledge in their drawings right from the beginning. They are sorting out what the lines and shapes stand for in the real world. We also saw that the meanings of the lines, and the way in which they are drawn, varies with context.

The stages of intellectual and visual realism may be more apparent than real. The use of statistical pictures of children's development, creates a stage-like illusion. Only detailed longitudinal studies reveal the truth. There are no stages in children's drawing development. It is a continuum which undergoes transformations woven together in dynamic, co-operating, perceptual-motor systems.

An important point has been that the act of drawing guides children's observation of the environment. This idea is the other way around from the idea that drawing is the result of somehow copying the shapes we see in the real world. In contrast, children start to notice shapes in the environment because of shapes which appear on the drawing surface. In a real sense, visual reality takes shape on the drawing surface. What we understand as the shapes of things is a product of the drawing systems, not a copy of a reality that exists independently of our forms of representation (Atkinson, 2002 forthcoming). This is important to grasp, because it means that children are able to draw from observation only in so far as the shapes they see in the real world are, in some ways, like the shapes in their drawings. The teaching implications of this are enormous. Simply forcing children to draw from life will not in itself speed up development. Indeed, my evidence and experience convince me that the reverse is true – premature instruction in drawing from observation damages development.

Different, converging influences lead Ben towards projective relationships and the beginnings of perspective in his drawings, so that he does not just use topological relationships. One way children move towards using perspective is through their symbolic play and their movement through the three dimensions of space and the dimension of time. To show a view of something on paper is as much to do with showing a particular moment in the flow of time as it is with drawing the object itself from a single viewpoint.

In play, the child constructs imaginary universes in which he or she moves through a variety of directions of movement. By rotating a handheld toy through a range of orientations and systematically taking a number of sightings of the object at different points in time and space, she builds up an understanding of what might be seen from different positions. How the child learns to represent events and objects in time and space on the two-dimensional surface is the subject of the next chapter.

What about the adult support for this? What can adults do to help? A great deal of nonsense is spoken these days about intervention, scaffolding and of focusing the child's attention. The subtle ideas of Vygotsky have been lost or hijacked by those who want to control our children's minds. For – here comes the crunch – a great deal of this process has to be both spontaneous and solitary. Interaction and support does not mean constantly talking to children about what they are doing and what they should be noticing. Sometimes, interaction means doing *nothing*. Stop trying to teach the child. Do not be a teacher (at least, not in today's terms) but, rather, a 'more experienced learner' (Geva Blenkin, 2001, personal communication), an intellectual guide and companion.

These subtle distinctions, once natural to 'good enough' parents (Winnicott, 1971, Bettelheim 1987), are in danger of being hopelessly lost these days. The systematic destruction of educational theory has ensured that the relationship between talking to children, giving them instructions, and simply leaving them alone, are purposely blurred in the planned demolition of learner-centred education starting from the late 1970s in England. As predicted by Blenkin, Kelly, Athey, Bruce and others, an emphasis on a shrunken definition of language and literacy shows signs of having undermined the very literacy learning these enforced curriculum changes were supposed to support. No amount of chanting your phonemes will help you understand the multilayered meaning of signs and symbols. Only representational investigation and play will help you do that.

6

Space and time

Space and time are aspects of the same reality. One of children's concerns in representation seems to be the co-ordination of these two aspects. In their play, painting and drawing, children make patterned sequences of movement which they realise share characteristics with patterns of movement they see in the outside world. In symbolic and representational play they enact movement passages in terms of both continuous trajectory (see Figure 55) and individual steps or displacements in time and space (see Figure 56). They think about and represent both configurative aspects and dynamic aspects of events. For example, the painting by Ben at age two years (Figure 57) records an aeroplane crashing to the ground, in terms of its continuous trajectory and point of arrival (action representation), as well as in terms of the shapes of the twisted wreckage (configurative representation). Figure 58 (by a Chinese Singaporean two-year-old) shows an imminent collision between a terrorist suicide plane and a tower building, in terms of the shapes of the objects involved (configurative representation) as well as in terms of explosive impacts (dynamic representation).

Children attend to a wide variety of unfolding phenomena. As we have seen, they think about complex patterns of movement like complex events, such as clouds moving, rain coming down or milk spilling from a cup, or simple trajectories and moments of impact like an aeroplane crashing. They represent such highly visible, catastrophic events, and also invisible ones like suction and wind, or subtle events like 'sitting.' Some of these events happen in the real world; some of these events they see on television or in the advertising media. Whichever is the case, they do not merely copy from their surroundings, but actively reconstruct events according to interests they themselves are generating. They pick and choose from surrounding culture, both from real events and society's pictorial world, including television and electronic media. But

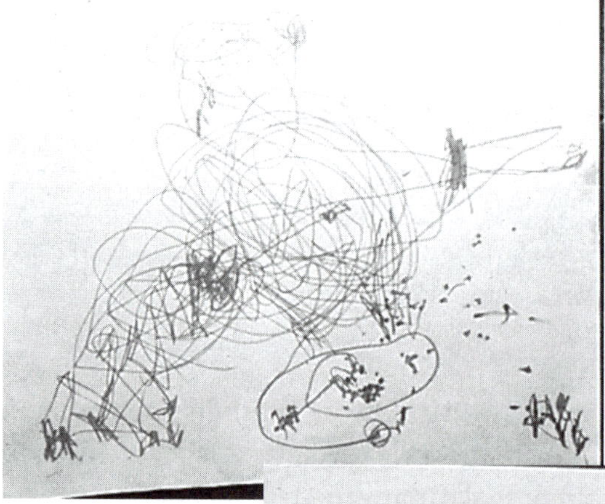

Figure 55   A continuous linear trajectory of an object. Joel, aged two years and two months, draws the flight of an aeroplane

Figure 56   Movement broken up into individual displacements in time and space. A painting by Ben, aged two years and four months

children do not select just anything and everything. They pick and choose from their surroundings, whether this be the physical environment or the pictorial one, and this selection is based upon interests they themselves are forming. This is the essential point for educators to understand.

These attractors or emergent concepts allow children to see the deep structures beyond surface appearance. They find the same dynamic structures beyond the superficial variation in content. One example would be the concept of 'going through', whether this be smoke or Father Christmas going through a chimney (Figures 54 and 79), or music going through a trumpet

Figure 57 A painting by Ben, aged two years and four months, shows the trajectory and impact of an aeroplane crashing. This is action representation. *Within the same painting he also shows the shapes of the tangled wreckage. This is* configurative representation

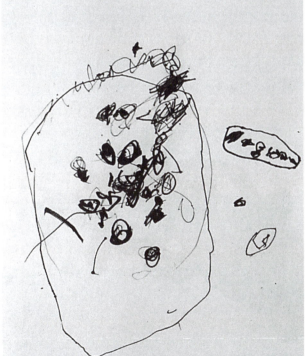

Figure 58 This drawing, by two-year-old See Kang Luo, shows the impending impact of a terrorist suicide plane into a tower building. This event is described in terms of the shapes of the objects involved (configurative representation) *and in terms of the explosive impacts* (action representation)

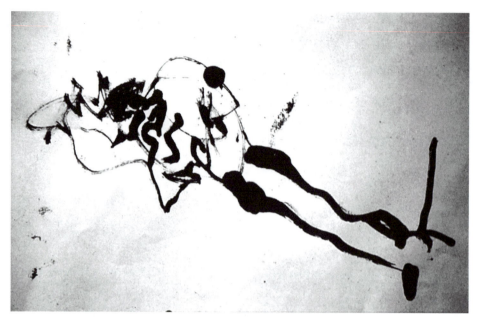

Figure 59   Ben, aged three years and one month, paints a tadpole figure

Figure 60   'Someone washing', says Ben about his next painting

(Figure 80 in Chapter 7), or light going through the lens of a camera (Chan and Matthews, 2002a).

We have seen how children's interest in changes of position and state often alternate with each other in quick succession. A good example of this is a series of paintings in black oil paint on paper which Ben produced at the age of three years and one month. Here we can see him moving in and out of a range of representational concerns, sometimes within a single painting.

In the first of the series, he paints a portrait of me, in tadpole form, in which those familiar, paired parallel lines represent my legs (see Figure 59). Feet are differentiated from the legs by marks attached at approximate right angles. The facial features are upside down with respect to the rest of the drawing. This tadpole figure shows the configurative aspect of representation – it is concerned with the shape of a person.

The next painting in the series is, he says, about 'someone washing' and starts off with a configurative representation at the bottom left, the shape of a water tap (see Figure 60). Perhaps he thought directly about the visual form of the tap, or perhaps he arrived at this shape by thinking about the action of the water running through it. Further to the right he changes to a quite different way of representation. A circular motion of the brush in a pool of paint shows the actions of 'someone washing'. This, then, is a movement, a dynamic representation. Further to the right he returns to a configurative representation when he runs those parallel grouped lines down into the pool of paint to show someone's arms reaching into the washbasin. Ben alternates between configurative and dynamic ways of representation within a single painting.

The third painting (see Figure 61) is of a helicopter. Who can say whether this represents the shape of the helicopter, or perhaps the dynamic action of its rotor blades? Or, perhaps in describing the action of the helicopter he arrives at something of its shape. This is part of the way painting and drawing work – not by somehow copying the world, but by generating a world within the act of painting itself.

In the last of the series (see Figure 62) he seems to relax momentarily from the struggle to master shapes. He now plays freely with shapes and lines on paper. New forms made in this free play will be carried back into his next attempts at representing the world. Dennie Wolf (1984) has described how playful ways of drawing and the struggle for mastering drawing flow into and nourish each other.

Ben is engaged in an ongoing conversation, in which marks and shapes appearing on the paper encourage him to think in certain ways about their

Figure 61   'A helicopter', by Ben, the third painting in the series

Figure 62   In the last of this series of four paintings, Ben free-plays with shapes and lines

relationships. Painting episodes can be likened to a journey into an ever-changing landscape in which, at every twist and turn, new vistas of possibilities emerge. From moment to moment, the marks on the paper prompt representational possibilities which the child pursues, but which are later overtaken by other possibilities suggested by newly appearing shapes and colours.

There are important implications here about visual and linguistic narrative. Telling stories in pictures appears throughout the history of art. Shortly we will see how Ben develops this in a series of drawings made over the next few months. This dialogue not only involves Ben's drawing; rather, his whole reality becomes the currency of this continuous fluid exchange. If we look at Ben's construction with blocks and Lego in the miniaturised world of symbolic play, we see him progressing from dynamic play (representing movement) to the configurative use of his schemas in which the shapes of things are represented.

The floor is strewn with wooden blocks and Lego, toy cars, toy people and drawing materials. At first glance it looks chaotic, but in fact there is an 'arrangement' which changes over the days. Ben is interested in fire at this time.

Ben represents many of the different forms which fire can take. Sometimes these are fierce conflagrations; aeroplanes crashing and bursting into flames or cars burning on the side of a hill. Or else, fire serves as the motive force of air or spacecraft. In Figure 63, he represents fire *going through* two parallel lines representing a spacecraft. Above it is his initial letter 'B'. The zigzag is 'writing' describing the drawing. This is around the time he is drawing other manifestations of 'going through', like smoke (or Father Christmas) going through a chimney. It is autumn and bonfires have appeared in the neighbourhood. Ben is only three years and three months, so, during the previous autumn he may have been too young to notice fires.

There may be a second level of symbolic meaning here. His themes of play at this time seem to revolve around the transmission and control of energy. It might involve line of sight, trajectory, moment of impact and explosions. It also manifests itself in gunplay. This might, for a three-year-old, make fire a highly salient image. This kind of play is the most seriously misunderstood aspect of representation, especially in boys' play. This mistake is disastrous to the development of representation. Until the play of boys and girls is studied carefully, in a non-partisan manner, great damage will be caused by ill-conceived ideas of social engineering coming from a predominately female workforce (Sumsion, 1999). It is true that uncared for children sometimes gain access to real guns and there are tragic consequences. However, while adults (and not just men) might mistake representation with reality, children do not.

Figure 63   Fire goes through two parallel lines representing a spacecraft. Above it is his initial letter – 'B'. The zigzag is 'writing' describing the drawing

Three-dimensional constructions: the relationship to two-dimensional work

One day, Ben gathers up armfuls of coloured plastic straws (actually a construction kit) and repeatedly throws them up in the air making fire noises. He is representing the dynamic aspect of the fire, the movement and the sound of brightly coloured flames leaping. Over a period of ten days he gradually introduces other objects to his heap of toys, including pieces of Lego and wooden blocks (see Figures 64 and 65).

'Heaping' objects is often the first way children classify objects (Athey, 1990), and Ben's use of the heap to represent a fire originates from this level. He continues to jumble up this collection into a constantly moving heap, to represent the constant motion of the fire. The 'fire' goes through a series of transformations during this period, as different elements are added or subtracted. At one time he uses a sleeping bag which he drags into the room.

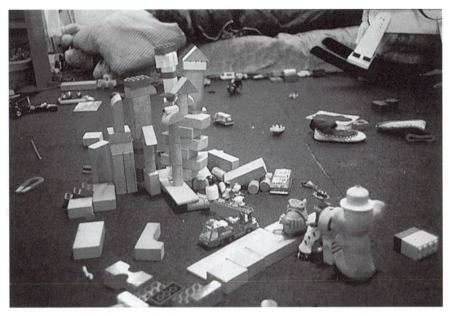

Figure 64   An early stage of a 'fire' built by Ben, aged three years and three months

This acts as a demarcated area for the fire. Gradually, the way he moves the blocks, changes. There is less jumbling and tumbling, more careful adjustment of pieces. Eventually, Ben modifies this heap of blocks, Lego and the few remaining plastic straws, as if it is a piece of sculpture.

While the fire moves through these continuous transformations, one thing in this play scenario changes only a little. Apart from a little daily variation, a line of cars and characters including a cowboy, Donald Duck, a plastic bear with a light 'rose' for a hat, and 'Squeaky Man' – a soft plastic toy who squeaks when you press him – all queue up to watch the fire (Figure 64). The fire is the central pivot which undergoes many massive transformations during a period of several days' play. This is a three-dimensional version of core and radial, the visual structure Ben uses in his drawing. During the last phase of this play, Ben makes carefully formed towers of blocks and Lego to represent, not buildings, but tongues of flame (see Figure 65).

This sculpture would have been impressive as a representation of a building, or simply in terms of balancing blocks upon one another. It is the fact that this sculpture represents something so ephemeral as a fire which makes it so especially interesting. Ben has used three-dimensional materials in a similar way to his use of two-dimensional media. He has been concerned both with the dynamic and configurative aspects of an event, fire. Over a

Figure 65 'The fire' at a later stage, by Ben, aged three years and three months

period of ten days, in a free-flow interaction between play with the materials and construction (Bruce, 1991), he has moved from a representation which captures the movement of the fire in time, to one which incorporates its form in space. The dynamic aspect of the schemas has guided and enriched the configurative aspects. In some ways, Ben's thinking is like that of a creative, adult thinker or artist, starting with a hazy, germinal sketch and moving through variations and possibilities, to its ultimate realisation in more concrete terms which incorporates all the main features about which the thinker has been concerned.

There are some important teaching implications to be noted here. First, a process of development has been allowed to take place over time. The majority of children rarely get this opportunity in conventional nursery and early years' settings. Secondly, the objects he uses are not always used for the purposes for which they were designed (by adults). The use of the construction kit of plastic straws is an example.

The functional categories between different kinds of object are transgressed. Different sets of objects have been mixed together. Household objects, including a mirror, a sleeping bag and a light 'rose', are mingled with manufactured toys. Together, everything is transformed into a toy universe. On one occasion, he finds a book on space travel in which there is a photograph of a rocket taking off, with jets of flame shooting from its combustion chamber. He opens the book at this page and lays it on the floor. Onto this two-dimensional image of the flames he then builds a three-dimensional formation of blocks, which again represents flames. Like nearly all other children at around this age, Ben is fully aware of the differences between images and solid forms. However, also like other children, he has no preconceptions about boundaries and conventions of representational systems, even between the two-dimensional and the three-dimensional (see Figure 66).

Figure 66   Three-dimensional flames are combined with two-dimensional flames using blocks and a picture in a book, by Ben, aged three years and three months

Ben is not unusual in this way, most children do this if they have the opportunity and are not discouraged from doing so. For example, in Singapore, Chinese three-year-olds were observed flying their drawings of aeroplanes through the air with handheld paper swooping through space.

However, this kind of thinking is not be possible if adults decide beforehand how the toys and books should be classified and used (much recent advice on 'focusing the child's attention' comes from such assumptions). Linda and I made no restriction on his use of media based on a prior classification of our own. We did not interfere with his combination of objects. Drawing materials have also been mixed in with his other toys. Every so often, he would stop building and draw. There was an interaction between his thinking in two-dimensions and his thinking in three-dimensions. More fundamental still is that, at this level, Ben's thinking is embedded in actions he performs on these objects of play. To tidy up these objects each day would have been to totally disrupt his flow of thinking. Linda and I cleared up around the sculpture, allowing the central formation to remain.

The ecology of creativity

The difficulties in allowing for this development in the classroom are exaggerated. All early years environments should be redesigned beyond the idea of mere housekeeping. I cannot write a book or make an artwork if I have to put everything away after an hour or so. If it is not possible to preserve the actual construction or sculpture, it is possible for the teacher to make a drawing of such a sculpture and to rebuild it later from this plan. Or Polaroid photographs or video recordings can be made and used as plans for rebuilding. This can form a powerful part of evaluation and pupil-profiling (Bartholomew and Bruce, 1993). More fundamentally, this recording and re-building from plans is, in itself, rich with teaching possibilities. Young children are intrigued by the fact that their work can be recorded in various forms and reconstructed. Children can learn to record their own work. Rebecca Chan and I have shown that two-year-olds can do this with video cameras. Perhaps, they may learn to reassemble their work from prior drawings. Note that this is not the same thing as requiring children to plan *before* they get their hands on materials, as is the case with High/Scope and other similar schemes (Hohmann, Banet and Weikart, 1979). Due to a tradition of academics who misunderstand and despise physical, sensory experience, and who devise educational curricula in favour of abstract, disembodied learning, this part of literacy remains neglected. The acts of playing, constructing and reconstructing from plans is the basis of 'reading' the world – and rebuilding it (Freire, 2000). It may be possible for children to learn to make plans prior to making things, but only after much practice with the possibilities of the materials. Being able to discuss, with another, what you are going to do, or are doing, is difficult for an adult artist (I cannot really explain my own work as an artist), so, to devise curricula in which such expectations are made of children is yet another form of institutionalised oppression.

There is one more, related point to make here. Provision for block play is often based on the assumption that it is a communal activity. Frequently, completely individual, personal construction is subjected to upheaval and destruction by adult teachers. If it is claimed that such processes of individual development cannot be accommodated in the nursery then some serious questions should be raised about the reason for early childhood education in the first place.

Showing more complex events in space and time

Here we will look at how Ben draws the relations between and within objects and events.

Figure 67   'The train goes "over" the bridge', by Ben, aged three years and three months

A drawing by Ben at age three years and three months (see Figure 54) is a good example. As always, my analysis is derived from what Ben actually told me about his drawing. It shows Father Christmas arriving on top of a house. He is shown in two positions in time and space. A closed shape represents the house. Ben has differentiated higher and lower relationships in the closed shape. A horizontal line subdivides it, representing the upper floor. Ben has, for several weeks, been showing higher and lower relations on the drawing surface – one example being his drawings in Figures 67 and 68, of which, he says, 'the train goes "over" the bridge' (Figure 67) and 'crashed "under" the bridge' (Figure 68).

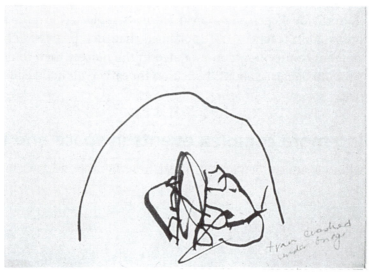

Figure 68 'The train crashed "under" the bridge', by Ben, aged three years and three months

The marking of higher and lower relations develops until it becomes a true vertical axis. This seems to be happening in Ben's drawing of the house with its 'upstairs' and 'downstairs', with the fireplaces on the lower and upper floors vertically in line with the chimney (Figure 54). Perhaps he is showing a cross-section or a totally foreshortened view of the upper floor. Remember my comments about foreshortened planes and sections, for example, in the drawing of the 'man digging in the ground for the bones of animals' (see Figure 50 in Chapter 5). Ben also shows a possible 'edge-on' or totally foreshortened view of a table-top upon which objects rest. There is a detail of this foreshortened view of the table-top in Figure 52 (also in Chapter 5).

Ben is not concerned with showing true angles in the boundaries of the house or in the corners of the table. We could look at Ben's drawing in terms of deficits but that would be to go against the principles of early childhood education (Bruce, 1987). Such a negative approach would show that Ben has failed to preserve the rectangularity of a 'real' house and of a 'real' table.

Adults working from a deficit theory approach might want to point out to a child the right angles in the 'carpentered environment', as in windows, doors and tables, with the aim of correcting these so-called 'errors'. Others might claim that this supposed inability is confounded by a difficulty in making right-angular line junctions. However, this would be to totally misconstrue the way Ben is making his representations. For a start, we can dismiss the claim that his drawing may be accounted for in terms of difficulty in making various line junctions. As we look around the different parts of the drawing, we find that certain objects have been composed of right-angular joins. We will return to these later. But, more fundamantally, Ben's concern is not with the Euclidean properties of the house. He represents the house as a volume which encloses people and furniture. To this basic *topological* geometry (Piaget and Inhelder, 1956; Willats, 1997; Tormey and Whale, 2002; Whale, 2002) he adds higher and lower relations to show that objects rest on tables, while the vertical linear relationship between the chimney and fireplaces allows Father Christmas to descend.

It is later on that he will use controlled angular variation or 'moments of turn' (Chris Athey, personal communication and Athey, 1990) in line junctions, when he feels it important to preserve the angular variation in, for example, the depiction of corners, and when he realises the significance of angular variation in letter and number forms. These Euclidean properties are not present overall in the drawing under discussion, and their occasional presence is not adequately explained by Piaget's stage theory of the development of geometrical systems (Willats, 1997).

Ben mixes geometrical knowledge which is essentially topological in character (inside-outside, boundary, closure, hollowness, connectivity), and dynamic knowledge (of the movement of objects from place to place, for example, Father Christmas), with other information which is Euclidean – that is, it captures the true shapes of objects and the angles at which lines are joined.

As I noted above, one popular explanation for the child's omission of accurate angles between lines has been that it is a problem of motor planning and control. It is often thought that very young children simply cannot attach lines to each other at the necessary angles. But this idea also does not bear scrutiny. For example, in certain parts of the drawing, Ben shows he is quite capable of forming right-angular junctions and parallel lines. The point is that he uses these junctions and structures to capture information which he feels is important but which an adult might not. For instance, he does not necessarily use these to show rectangular, 'carpentered' features, for corners of the table and so on. The important information about the table is that there are Christmas packages 'on top of' it. However, he does use parallels and approximate right-angular junctions to show things and events which are important to him. A good example is near the bottom of the drawing where Linda is shown vacuuming the floor. A small piece of paper is about to be sucked up into the vacuum cleaner. It is possible that Ben uses the parallel grouped lines at the base of the vacuum cleaner to represent the invisible action of suction.

Going through a bound volume

Ben represents another movement through a tube; Father Christmas's entry and descent through a chimney. Ben is thinking of the different positions in both space and time. We can see Father Christmas in Position 1, on his sleigh and, a moment later, in Position 2, about to descend the chimney. We need to remember that we are looking at just one individual person, Father Christmas, and not two people. He is being shown at two different moments in time as well as space. So this drawing is very complex in terms of Ben's understanding and organisation of events and objects occurring within space and time. He has obviously thought about the actual house in which he hopes this event will take place, and has found out something about its geometry. When he plays the adventures of Father Christmas – his journey through the sky onto the roof and his descent through the chimney – this helps him build up and co-ordinate the understandings of time and space which make this drawing possible. I discussed emergent aspects of this, earlier on in the book in the way children are fascinated with the beginnings and endings in time and space. When children make dots and blobs in a line (see Figure 56 in Chapter 6), or hop along the ground in games, or pretend to be rabbits hopping (Wolf and Fucigna, 1983), or hold miniature people and jump them up and down along a line to represent their footsteps, they are using actions and objects to show sequences in time and space.

Movement and time: changes of state and changes of position

This concern with the passing of time in space is re-explored all over again at different moments in the child's life. A good example of this is Ben's 'King and castle' series. In the drawing which he says is about a 'king falling off a castle' (see Figure 69), the unfortunate man topples from the top of the castle, falling in stages until his impact with the ground is marked with a dynamic squiggle of the pen. As he falls, he loses his crown on the way. Ben is clearly trying to co-ordinate and represent the flight-paths or trajectories of two objects which start off their descents together but which then follow separate destinies.

Figure 69 'The king falls off a castle', by Ben, aged three years and three months

As the days pass, Ben continues to think about the king's movements. On another day, in another drawing, the king goes for a walk up the hill and retrieves a flying kite (Figure 70). This is almost the reverse condition, because now, the two separate trajectories converge. On another day, in another drawing, the king jumps off the castle and goes for a walk (Figure 71). This is one of the recurring themes of his play and drawings during these weeks. The drawings are in fact stimulated by a toy he has at this time which consists of a set of plastic cups graded in size so that the entire set can either be nested concentrically within the largest or, with the largest inverted and forming a base, the other cups can be placed rim down on each other from bigger to smaller to form a tower. The final and smallest item, which can either be contained at the centre of the concentrically nested cups, or placed on top of the

Figure 70 'The king walks up a hill and catches a flying kite', by Ben, aged three years and three months

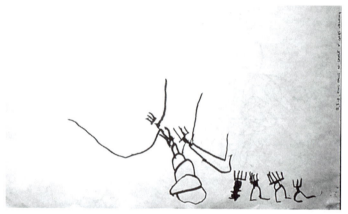

Figure 71 'The king jumps off the castle and goes for a walk', by Ben, aged three years and three months

tower, is a small plastic tube, closed at both ends and embossed with a face and a crown – the king. In play, Ben uses this handheld king to act out various flight-paths. He also used other towers, built with wooden blocks. A range of different types of trajectory was investigated with handheld toy figures around these towers. These imaginative play scenarios would flow back and forth between the two-dimensional environment of the drawing surface and the three-dimensional world of his pretend play (Bruce, 1991).

Sequences of events: visual narrative

An interesting drawing made by Ben at the age of three years and three months (Figure 72) shows his journey from nursery school to his house. Ben's

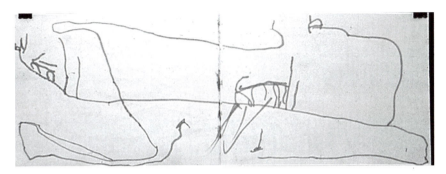

Figure 72 The journey from nursery school to home, by Ben, aged three years and three months

concern to mark the beginning and end of a linear route has been shifted here to a new level in his thinking. At the right-hand end of the line, a small closure represents the nursery school. We travel along this line, which represents a road, to Position 1, where Ben and Linda's standing figures are depicted, together with the pram which contains his baby brother, Joel. We continue along the road to the left, crossing the railway line, up a very steep hill, past the road which leads to the nurses' flats, to where the family and pram are shown in Position 2. From there we travel to the end of the line, where our house is demarcated.

Everything drawn showing the sequence of his route is correct. Ben also shows knowledge of the relationship of this route to other routes. The drawing has geographic as well as narrative aspects. The railway line over which the road crosses is part of the route from London to Liverpool to see his grandparents. Around this time Ben is producing map-like drawings of this journey in its entirety. It is worth noting that in many of these maps, the line wriggles around the paper surface in a circuitous, continuous sequence of folds. Ben knows that, in reality, the railway line between London to Liverpool has nowhere near so many bends. The track is generally straight. However, in a continuous action representation, he squeezes as much space and time into the confines of the available drawing surface. Concertinaed in this way, the line preserves the continuity of the journey rather than its Euclidean aspects (see Figure 51 in Chapter 5).

A few days later he produces a drawing which shows a flying boat taking off out of water (see Figure 73). A line shows the surface of the water. Ben might want to show the boundary between the surface of water and medium of air. The closed shape drawn above this line represents a boat (perhaps shown in section) taking off out of the water and flying into the air. Ben has repeated

Figure 73   At three years and three months, Ben draws a flying boat moving through four positions in time and space

the image four times on the same sheet of paper to show it moving through Positions 1 to 4. 'It takes time', is his explanation to me for drawing four images of the same object. From the base of each of the four drawings of the same boat are those roughly parallel grouped lines like the ones we saw when he showed paper being sucked into the vacuum cleaner. In this drawing they represent streams of water trailing off as this mysterious sailing boat ascends.

Co-ordinating horizontals and verticals

Interestingly, in Position 4, to the furthest right-hand side of the drawing surface, the boat has been rotated through 90 degrees so that the trails of water (grouped parallels) run out horizontally and stop in a right-angular junction with the last vertical line of the preceding boat's water trails.

There are various possible interpretations of this part of the drawing. Piaget and Inhelder (1956) would say Ben cannot show different parts of the drawing in a co-ordinated way – he cannot fit everything into an Euclidean co-ordinate system of horizontals and verticals. Or another, slightly different, interpretation is that Ben cannot combine thinking about the top–bottom relationship in a detail of the picture, with a larger, all-encompassing top–bottom relationship. In their studies, Piaget and Inhelder showed children line drawings of upright and tilted containers and studied how the children drew the water-level inside these drawings of containers. They also studied how the children aligned trees on the side of a drawn outline of a hillside. Sensitive studies by Gavin Bremner (1985) suggest that young children may understand horizontals and verticals in the real world, but have difficulty drawing these due to the powerful visual effects of lines and line junctions which arise during the drawing process. However, none of these studies is about children's spontaneous drawing, so they are insufficient as explanations for real-life situations. They do not sufficiently address the issues which Willats's (1992; 1997) work has highlighted, namely the constraints and possibilities of the drawing medium. Typically, such experiments involve either adding something to someone else's drawing, or copying a drawing. They do not help us to understand the children's spontaneous drawings.

In their spontaneous drawings, children make decisions about visual structure from moment to moment in free-flowing play with the drawing medium (Bruce, 1991). The drawing is a fluid episode in which the *denotational* values of lines (what the lines represent) are indeterminate or ambiguous (Willats, 1985; 1997). What the lines stand for, changes from moment to moment. Hence, as Ben draws the lines representing water trails from the bottom of Boat 4, they terminate at a convenient baseline which, only moments before, served to represent another trail of water from Boat 3.

It is consistent with this way of thinking that Ben does not consider the finished drawing as a whole or from a single viewpoint. Since the water has to fall from the bottom of the boat, then this remains the rule for boat in Position 4 – even though it is turned on its side. This might involve the object-centred type of information we mentioned earlier and it might implicate language, that is, verbal descriptions of objects which include terms like 'top' and 'bottom'. It might mean that these different attractor systems (including linguistic, visual, haptic and dynamic 'knowledge' about the subject) are not yet overlapped and conjoined. Another possibility is that Ben is showing how trails of water might be left behind in space as the boat turns on its side and flies off at speed. It may be that during his play in the bath, Ben learnt about water-lines and how water drips or pours from handheld boats flying in space.

None of these explanations are mutually exclusive. As Nancy Smith (1983) has remarked, the beginnings of representation might be necessarily amorphous to allow for the proliferation of symbolic thought.

Children learn from other people's pictures

Another influence upon this and other serialised images he drew was the comic books he avidly studied at this time. In particular, he was interested in the 'Rupert' picture-story books. In one of these adventures, the great English artist, Alfred Bestall, illustrates, in a sequence of 'stills' or 'frames', a special boat taking off from a lake. Water does indeed trail off from the bottom of the boat. However, these pictures of a sailing yacht differ fundamentally from the ones Ben produces. Ben did not 'copy' Bestall's pictures but 'filtered' them, as it were, through developing schemas, which are attracted to certain types of structure in both three-dimensional and pictorial environments. I used to think of these like mental templates but this does not capture their dynamic, self-generating and renewing aspect. We shall return to this important point again as it will help to understand the processes involved when children are taught or influenced.

Talking to children about how pictures work

From about the age of one Ben enjoys looking at picture stories with me. At around two and a half years of age he is clearly trying to work out the conventions of the serialised-image mode. He asks questions like, 'Why is there more than one Rupert?' I explain that there is really only one Rupert but that the first picture shows Rupert setting off from his mummy's and daddy's house and the next picture shows him a little later on when he has reached another place.

Ben is extremely interested in these explanations. The conversations form part of a very important interaction between Ben, myself and Linda in which we discuss how pictures work, both his own and those of other people. This dialogue helps him to talk about his own ways of drawing. It helps him to gain more control and freedom in his drawing since he is being helped to think about how his drawings work. The unfolding nature of children's drawing development, while self-generated, does require a special kind of interaction with other people as well as provision of materials if it is to fully flourish. This interaction includes pictures by other artists and discussions about how these work. As Ben grows older, further conversations with him about his own pictures and those of other artists help him to develop his techniques in drawing and painting.

Unfortunately there are indications recently that ideas about interaction are being distorted by poor interpretation of key concepts. I referred above to the misuse of crucial terms in early years education, and the subtle but insidious distortion of ideas about interaction and support. It is worth giving a reminder here. For a start, this interaction does not necessarily or solely have to be in verbal language. Nor does it mean taking over the child's work or requiring her to adhere to a list of instructions. Sometimes a conversation between adult and child might naturally ensue about the child's art. Sometimes a very few words go a long way. At other times, not a word need be spoken.

Many different pictures from a few drawing rules

Emergent concepts about changes of states and changes of position seem to form the deep structures underlying much of Ben's drawing at this time. With great enthusiasm, he draws and paints the shapes of events as well as the shape of objects. His drawings of serialised images are interspersed with other fascinating drawings of a wide range of subject matter. Yet, in formal terms, he has at his disposal a quite limited vocabulary of drawing devices. He is able to employ his same small repertoire of lines and shapes by making subtle modifications depending on what he is drawing. Again, this under-lines how important it is, when considering how a drawing is made, to also consider the content, because these interact together. What Ben draws will affect how he uses the rules he knows about drawing.

The drawing shown in Figure 74 is by Ben, aged three years and three months. It is a representation of an astronaut's footprint on the Moon. At the

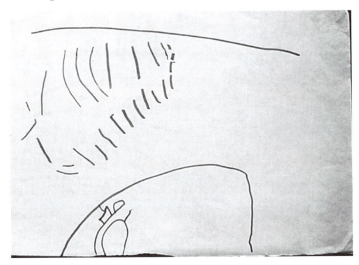

Figure 74 'Footprints of a monster on the moon', by Ben, aged three years and three months

Figure 75 'Red Indians in the long grass with flags', by Ben, aged three years and three months

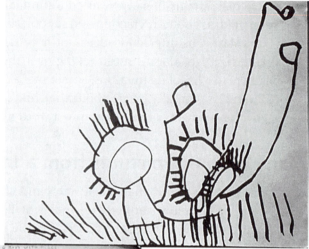

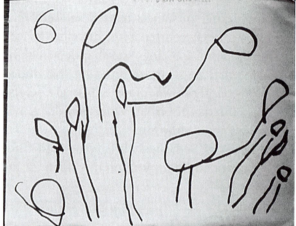

Figure 76 'Six boys with flags', by Ben, aged three years and three months

Figure 77 'Red Indian chief shooting lots of arrows', by Ben, aged three years and three months

bottom of the drawing, a figure looks up through a transparent dome at this image of the boot's tread-mark. He saw the famous photograph of the first person's footprint on another world in a space-travel book in a public library. He was immediately struck by this powerful image. 'What's that?' he asked me. He recognised it readily enough when I explained it was a footprint. He asked further questions and I tried my best to explain. This involved concepts which are quite difficult for an adult, let alone a three-year-old, to comprehend. Ben knew about footprints, and he also knew about the Moon. How could a footprint get on the Moon? The other photographs in the book showed the astronauts themselves, walking on the Moon's dust. Perhaps to a three-year-old, these figures, transformed by their white spacesuits, do not look like humans at all. When Ben made the drawing at home, he said that it was a 'footprint of a monster on the Moon'.

Over a period of a few weeks, from the age of three years and two months (when he drew the drawing of Linda in her dungarees) to three years and five months, Ben produces a profusion of fascinating drawings of people we now call Native North Americans, including, 'Red Indians in the long grass with flags' (Figure 75), 'Six boys with flags' (Figure 76) and 'A Red Indian chief shooting lots of arrows' (Figure 77). It is remarkable that all of these drawings are composed using the same drawing rules described above:

- closure;
- variations on right-angular joints;
- core and radial units;
- U shape on baseline;
- parallel grouped lines;
- zigzags, waves and loops;
- energetic squiggles.

This is the sum total of the shapes and lines he possesses. The same ones are used by most three- and four-year-olds. What makes Ben's drawings unusual is the way he varies, modifies and combines these forms. It is the imaginative way he brings them together which gives the drawings their power and seemingly endless permutations. In Ben's drawing, the meaning of the lines and how they are produced, in terms of variations of pressure, speed and intensity, changes drastically according to context. Closed shapes have been used for a variety of faces, both of objects and people, or to convey volumetric solids in their entirety. Single lines have stood for boundaries of volumes, or as cracks, wires, straps, streams of water or as tubular volumes, like arms. They have also been used to suggest imaginary lines like water-lines and sections through the ground. By varying parallel grouped lines just slightly, or joining them at varying angles to a baseline, they have been used to represent the legs of animals or people, points of crowns or straps of dungarees. They have been used to represent the boundaries of tubular volumes like trumpets and chimneys and human bodies. They have been used to denote the tread-mark of an astronaut's boot, Native American headdresses, long grass, even the flow of water and air. This list is by no means exhaustive.

The uses and variations of right-angles are numerous. It is an extremely effective way of creating differences and contrast between shapes. There is a special kind of right angle used in the core and radial unit. Using this form, children are able to show the relationship between roundish volumes and long, tubular or stick-like ones. The tadpole figure and the Sun are only two of the many examples of this relationship. Water dripping from flying boats is a more unusual example. Another variation of right-angular attachment is the U shape on baseline. Like basic closed shapes, it can be used to contain other elements, such as a house which contains people. By joining such U shapes together in various ways one can generate a range of cell-like units.

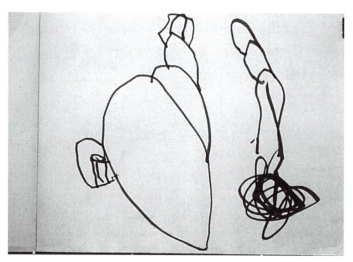

Figure 78   A tower (to the left) next to a rocket-ship taking off. Both are composed from U shape on baseline, in this case with U shape attached to preceding U shape, by Ben, aged three years and three months

U shapes can be clustered together to form complex houses or vehicles (see Figure 78) or placed on top of each other to form towers off which kings can topple.

Ben has an ability which he shares with some, but not all, very young draughtspersons. He can approach the same or similar forms with a variety of strategies. He has plenty of choice as to how to go about drawing something. One example is the various ways he can make closures and add them together, either by using the basic closed shape, or by using a U shape on baseline, or a travelling loop, like an elegant 'e' or '6'. Each of these is slightly different but they can all be used to arrive at a similar end. Although other writers have stressed the habitual structural preferences in young children's drawing, given the right environment, children are not nearly so stuck in certain drawing routines as is sometimes supposed. Like many other children, Ben can attach different lines to each other at any angle he wishes, using separated drawing actions. Or else he can make linear direction changes within a continuous contact of the pencil to paper, stopping a line at a certain position and starting it off again in a new direction. He can vary the speed of these angular variations. It is this ability to make controlled variations as he draws lines, which helps him to capture either the smoothly undulating forms of reindeers' antlers or else their spikiness.

Education and childcare: what we can do to help

The fact that Ben had a natural inclination to draw and paint should not be taken to mean that other children cannot achieve a similar fluency in drawing and painting. Just as important as naturally inherited traits, or parents who draw and paint, is the quality of interaction between caregiver and child. Most young children generate the visual structures I have so far described. Ben is a little unusual in that he combines these structures in such a large number of ways. However, my work in Singapore and London has convinced me that the ability to so conjoin different structures in a variety of ways is as much the product of an intelligent learning environment as it is of genetic inheritance. Children need the opportunities and the permission to be allowed to make these associations. If these are not recognised as meaningful but discouraged by teachers, then the ability to generate new families of visual structure will die out. In turn, this will affect the child's ability to make cross-references between different forms of knowledge.

Linda and I tried to talk intelligently with Ben about how his drawing worked. What is required is an interest and understanding of child development and an interest in the arts. It is far more important as a caregiver to have an understanding of how art processes might promote development in a child than to possess artistic skills oneself. Linda and I did what other people can do – create a field of discourse, an area of shared understanding about form, shape, colour and meaning, which permeated all our actions and conversations.

My experience of working and playing with children other than my own, in London and Singapore nursery classes, is that they are often delighted to find that it is actually possible to talk about drawings in a serious way, which goes beyond the 'very nice' response. It is possible to interact with children in a way which will help them understand, at a more conscious level, how forms interact to create meaning. In order to achieve this, it is necessary that teachers, parents and other caregivers have knowledge about what is available within a human discipline (be it mathematics, language or art) and how this interacts with processes of human development. With this approach it is quite possible for teachers and parents to create environments in which both children and adults are immersed in ideas about structure, form and content; environments where it is understood and accepted that one has the freedom and the right to experiment with relationships of shape, form and colour as signifiers of meaning and emotion.

It is certainly not the case that, as far as drawing and painting are concerned, 'one either has it or one hasn't'. There are ways to help enrich most children's abilities to formulate and manipulate images, and they need not be very complicated. Take what appears to be a fairly trivial response by a tired teacher to a child drawing: 'That's a very exciting zigzag line, Jason.' While this might sound banal, the teacher has communicated to the child:

- an interest in what he is drawing;
- a descriptive term for the type or class of line he has drawn; and
- an additional noun-qualifier which shows the child that this particular zigzag line has the power to excite.

Even from a trite comment like this, the child is learning about the multilayering of meanings in semiotic systems. This means that the child is being introduced, not only to the idea that lines and marks belong to geometrical, mathematical classes but (as Nick McAdoo pointed out to me in conversation), in addition, they have expressive attributes which cannot be mathematically described but which belong to the realm of aesthetics.

The problem for teachers and other adults is not one of just learning what to say, but of learning to see – and of seeing without prejudice. Developmental theory helps. Once you can see, you will know what to say. It is not even the case that one always has to say anything. Burying children with words is the very last thing one should do (Bruce, 1991). As to our understanding of children's development, as Dennis Atkinson (2002 forthcoming) points out, ultimately, development is indescribable. Our descriptions will always be provisional truths. But if the teacher has a genuine interest in the child's art, and a willingness to learn about it, this will communicate itself to the child. This sincere engagement will open up discourse with children, helping them develop a particular mode of thinking which is called *metacognition* – the ability to think about one's own thinking. It helps the child understand how she understands. This is true of thinking about and using form, shape, colour, line and action. More fundamentally, it is part of what it means to be literate. Sometimes an encouraging sound or gesture from the teacher is sufficient, for this will convey a wealth of shared understandings. There really are no absolute rules here – though this is a fact of life that many find hard to understand. Sometimes it is even necessary to pretend that one is not interested in a particular child's drawing because one knows that the slightest show of interest is likely to disrupt the child. In such cases, of course, it is still necessary to observe and record. It depends on the relationship of trust and understanding which has developed between children and teacher. The best teachers relate to very young children as fellow learners. A teacher is an adult companion to the child on an intellectual adventure.

Another way for adults to interact with children as they draw and paint is to be practically involved in painting and drawing too. But there is an inherent danger in this advice. The teachers who practise the most 'hands-on' type of interaction are often, paradoxically, those who are the most rigid and limited in their understanding of the arts. Being ignorant about art (or anything else) is not a crime. However, being unwilling to learn about it from children is. It is grossly insensitive to manipulate and interfere with children's work, sticking things on it, cutting it up, repainting it and generally communicating to the child that her efforts are inadequate. Such teachers often adopt a highly prescriptive approach, with a fixed end in mind (and often of the most banal kind). With these methods, children are reduced to slaves in a 'cottage-industry' production line, mass-producing stereotyped trivia (Athey, 1990; Bruce, 1991). This completely cuts across vital processes of symbol formation within the children. The English National Curriculum in Art has exacerbated the problem, because, though this replaces Christmas angels and Mother's Day cards with 'basic art elements' and 'direct experience' (still-life drawing), these and other components are similarly bolted together in an arbitrary way

(Matthews, 2001b). Although, since the first edition of my book, the National Curriculum has been modified many times (as its tottering architecture is hastily patched up) it remains, for the developing child, at best, just surviv-able; at worst, a form of child abuse. Unfortunately, at the present time, with governments obsessed with social control, a tight grip on the way children and adults represent the world is pervasive. While, on the one hand, govern-ments tend to push art to the periphery of the curriculum, as if it is of little importance, the truth is that governments always have had, and have now more than ever, a desire to tighten the grip on how children represent expe-rience. It matters not a jot whether the art curriculum is expressed in old-fash-ioned or traditional terms of visual realism, or in super-cool, postmodern terms; while it focuses on the transmission of a body of knowledge rather than on the development of modes of representation unfolding within the child, it will always be damaging to development. This type of approach has nothing whatsoever to do with the interaction I am advocating.

Unfortunately, a feminist misreading of the nature of boys' play has helped the destruction of representational skills. Mistaking it for the beginnings of male hegemony and violence, essential play involving lines of sight, trajectory and moment of impact (also present in girls' play but unnoticed by the female workforce who dominate early years education) have been banned from early childhood centres and nurseries (see Sumsion, 1999; Matthews, 2001c).

Summary

From three years and two months of age, Ben modifies and adapts a small number of shapes and lines in order to co-ordinate complex relationships in space and time in his pictures.

Like most other children, he uses systems which allow him to represent the structure within and between objects, as well as their movement. He plays with blocks and Lego and this helps him think about, and represent, the dynamic and configurative aspects of objects and events, their movement and their shape. He subdivides closed shapes to show higher and lower rela-tionships. He shows directions and successive stages of movement across, up, down, in space and time, or sometimes through a bound volume (such as a chimney, or a trumpet). He shows on-top-of relationships and creates fore-shortened or 'edge-on' views of objects (such as tables or antlers). This means that he is starting to organise representations of objects and their movements within three dimensions of space, plus the dimension of time.

Again, language is involved. The pictures are accompanied by Ben's spoken narrative. Language helps organise the drawing but, in turn, the drawing is extending his language. It may be that both language and drawing, along with other forms of representation, share the same basis in dynamic body movements (Allott, 2001). This may not be exactly what Piaget intended by a general 'semiotic function', rather, that the structures of language, symbols and signs originate from a deep '4 dimensional language' (Petitto, 1987), reflecting the dynamic systems which produced it.

During this prolific period of drawing, Ben generates images in which the lines and shapes stand for objects and events in the world. These lines and shapes transform the real world into shapes on the surface of a sheet of paper. However, they do not all do this in the same way. As we have seen, some visual processes represent the shapes of objects, some record the shapes of events. In the next chapter I shall discuss yet another kind of image he produces on the drawing surface, in which objects and events are represented not in terms of their shape, but in quite a different way.

7

The origin of literacy: young children learn to read

We have seen that children produce shapes on paper, which define the shapes of objects. We have also seen children use drawing to represent the movements of objects. Another kind of action is also represented in drawing. Very young children start to realise that they can represent, with their own marks on paper, the sounds of their own voices and the speech of others. We have seen some examples of this already, where Hannah counted her own drawing actions or made vocalisations in time with her drawing movements, or when Ben drew music going through a trumpet (see Figure 80).

Very young children look for the deep structures which persist despite changes in surface appearance. For example, if smoke, or Father Christmas

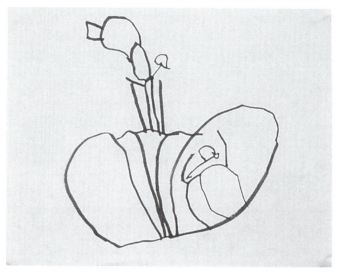

Figure 79 A drawing by Ben, aged three years and three months. Father Christmas going down and through the chimney, from outside the house to inside. Lower-case 'b' for 'Ben' (lower right) represents 'Ben in bed'

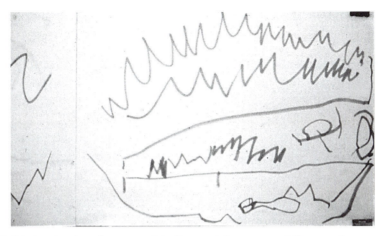

Figure 80 'Music going through a trumpet', by Ben, aged three years and three months

can go through a chimney (Figure 79) then music can go through a trumpet (Figure 80).

Another example is when Hannah, aged two years and two months, starts a drawing game with me in which she synchronises her own speech sounds, 'Baa-baa-baa', with intense horizontal arcing motions, moving a felt-tip pen from side to side. Analysis of the slow-motion video recording shows that each mouth-opening 'Baa' coincides almost precisely with the arcing strokes of the pen. Each marking action unit 'goes with' each vocal unit. Are we entitled to say that each arcing stroke *represents* each 'Baa'? What qualities do the vocalisations and the drawn horizontal arc share? Is she recording or 'writing down' each 'Baa' sound?

She then requests me to join in and, after I make the sounds, 'Baa-baa-baa', she makes three fanning movements of the pen. This is repeated several times, with Hannah maintaining a perfectly timed, rhythmic game of patterned interaction. It is almost as if she is writing down the words I am dictating.

B is Ben

In Figure 79 we can see images which, though made out of similar shapes, represent the world in rather different ways. To the left of the drawing we can see Father Christmas coming down the chimney. On the right, Ben is lying in bed. Ben is composed of a lower case 'b' – 'b' for 'Ben', meaning that Ben is in bed. Father Christmas is represented in a different way from that in which Ben is represented. Appreciating subtle differences – and connections

– between symbol and sign is vital if we are to understand children's development. We are required to 'read' each image in a different way.

- *Symbols*. The image of Father Christmas belongs to a category of symbols which capture something of the shape of the represented object. Adopting Piaget's definitions, I will call these visual or pictorial symbols. They include a wide range of pictures of objects and scenes.
- *Signs*. A rather different way in which reality can be represented is with the kind of image I will call signs. These include letters, words and numbers. These shapes do not physically resemble the things they represent.

However, although many traditional accounts of the verbal language often insist that letter and word shapes are arbitrary and conventional (as compared with pictures or symbols), the distinction between symbols and signs is not straightforward. It turns out that speech and human action share a deep language of motorpatterns (Allott, 2001; Bruce, 1987; Athey, 1990). Although it is undeniable that words – written or spoken – seem very different from the things they represent, there may still be some natural links between them. However, it is true to say that the way in which we learn how to read signs (letter, forms, numbers, mathematical signs) is different from the way we 'read' pictures. Though they share the same background in human perception, drawings specify forms and relations to the human brain in a different way than do words and sentences, I can look at the drawing to the left in Figure 81 and see a horse, but unless I have been taught the meaning of the English word 'horse', no amount of staring at the word 'horse' (to the right of Figure 81) will enable me to see the animal. This might seem glaringly obvious but remember that the child is encountering these different symbol systems for the first time, and has the task of working out (usually by herself, with no help), how, in their different ways they come to 'mean'.

The difference between symbol and sign is not always easy to see. Neither is the way symbols and signs correspond to reality. Characters of the Chinese Mandarin language, for example, started off thousands of years ago as pictures of the objects they represented and to this day still preserve something of their pictorial origins. The Mandarin character 'ma' (Figure 81, in the middle) is somewhere in between the more conventionalised English sign 'horse' and my drawing of a horse. However, the gap between these systems may not be as unbridgeable as I originally thought and it is probably within this gap that children do their most important investigation of semiotic systems. Young children use drawing to sort out both the differences and similarities

Figure 81   Three ways of representing 'horse'. On the left, a drawing of a horse; in the middle, the Chinese Mandarin character for 'horse' ('ma') and on the right, the English word 'horse'

between how symbols and signs work, and how they correspond to the world. They investigate how it is that objects and events plus sounds that we make can all be represented in two-dimensional shapes on paper.

Ben is now able to draw the closed loop mentioned earlier. This has alerted him to the existence of looped shapes of many kinds in the visual environment, including 'b', '6' and 'e'. As with most children, the image of his initial letter is especially significant to him. He, like other children, has incorporated this letter into his play world. In this drawing (Figure 79), a human made from a letter, and a human made of a visual symbol have equal representational status. The closed shape of the 'b' is even drawn resting on another closed shape which represents a pillow! Ben is resting, on a pillow, in bed. Though the two closed shapes which represent head and pillow are very similar in terms of pen-drawn shapes, how each corresponds to the real world is different. How far is Ben aware of this difference?

Of course, asking this begs the next question of how far do adult linguistic experts understand it (Deterding, 2002, personal communication)? Many researchers in emergent or developmental writing say that young children simply know the difference between pictures and words. This is clearly too crude. There is a time when children investigate how different visual structures work. It is as if they are working out how these different images can carry meaning. Piaget noted that, for the very young child, the word for an object was somehow in, or part of, the object. At present, Piaget's work on

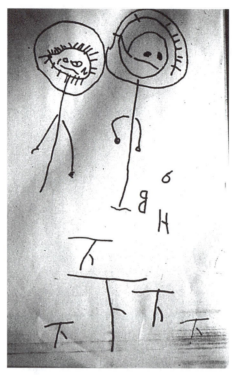

Figure 82 A four-year-old Chinese Singaporean learns how to make an oblique line junction. This alerts her attention to shapes in the environment, including arms which slope down from bodies, and the oblique line in the Mandarin character 'xia' which means 'down', or 'below' (at the lower part of the drawing)

language is unfashionable but he was right about the important relationship for a child, between an object and its name. In order for children to investigate these relationships, it is necessary for them sometimes to stretch the boundaries between what to adults might seem, on the one hand, arbitrary, conventional signs and what, on the other, seem to be pictorial symbols. They need to test the limits of meaning of symbols and signs. I believe this is what Ben, and many other children the world over, are doing in the drawings of early childhood. See, for example, Figure 82. Here we see two figures, with core and radial heads. Notice that the lines representing their arms slope downward. Now look at the Chinese characters to the lower right. This is the character 'xia', which means 'down' or 'below', in Chinese Mandarin. Note the downward oblique line in this character, crucial to encoding and decoding its meaning. Compare this with the oblique attachment of arms which

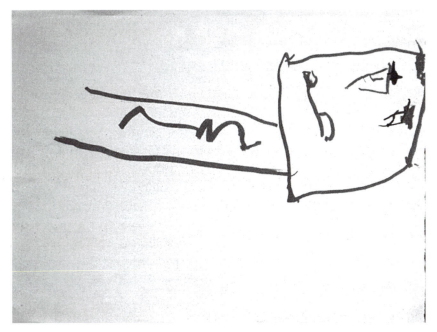

Figure 83 'Three astronauts in a spacecraft', by Ben, aged three years and three months

also slope 'down'. In Chinese writing, and in other writing systems in the world, we can still see the dynamic and perceptual basis for what are sometimes assumed to be arbitrary and conventionalised sign systems. Being Singaporean, this child also has to differentiate and see the relationship between figurative images, characters and yet another sign system, the Roman alphabet (because children are expected to learn English in Singapore).

In Figure 83, a rectangular closed shape represents a spacecraft, inside of which are three astronauts. Two of these are visual symbols for humans. He draws one astronaut in yellow and superimposes on his head a green helmet, and he draws the other in green and superimposes on his head a yellow helmet. Thus, in two senses of the word, the helmet 'covers' the head. This neat alternation of colour-coding helps us to appreciate the strong pictorial basis for these drawn people but also shows that pictures and the act of picturing implicate actions and language. The figure of Ben, the third astronaut, is represented by using a different sign system, the upper case 'B' for Ben! Yet both symbols and signs coexist with equal status in this two-dimensional environment.

The development of images and words, in both history and in individual human growth, are inextricably woven into each other. Anna Stetsenko writes that the drawing surface may be the best place for the child to discover what Vygotsky terms the 'dual function' of symbols and signs (Stetsenko, 1995).

Starting to read and write

Children, when they start to read and write, find the letters of their own names very significant, and they tend to interpret these as visual symbols, incorporating them into their drawings alongside more pictorial images. In Figure 53 (in Chapter 5), Father Christmas and his reindeer are flying over a house in which the letters 'B-e-n' are drawn inside a closed shape representing the house, meaning 'Ben is in the house'. Sometimes in early writing, letter forms are reversed or inverted. There are several reasons why this happens. The orientation of a letter or number shape on the page may not strike the child as particularly significant. After all, it is still possible to recognise drawings of objects even if they are rotated through 180 degrees (Temple, Nathan and Burris, 1982). Another factor is that very young children may not plan ahead in their writing, so, where they start determines how their letter shape is to continue. The same applies to some early drawings. In fact, Ben at three years and six months could startle us by seemingly effortlessly copying a picture completely back to front. This apparent ease may be linked with the hemispherical neural wiring, still in the process of completion, within the brain (Eliot, 1999). Later on he will not make these left/right flips. But left/right, top/bottom drawing reversals are not restricted to children, so may not be solely maturational but patterns of action triggered into motion with novel drawing or writing experiences. For example, when I wrote the first edition of this book I had started learning Mandarin and I sometimes made left/right reversals with Chinese characters. Now, several years later, I no longer make such reversals and would, in fact, find it difficult to purposely write them 'backwards'.

In Figure 84, letter forms at the bottom of the drawing 'describe' what is going on in Ben's drawing and, to the upper right, another house contains letters of names which stand for the people in the house. There is a fascinating fusion of numbers and visual symbols in Figure 76 (in Chapter 6); Ben draws 'six boys with flags'. There are six figures of boys in the drawing, and their flags are made out of 6s! This defies easy explanation but it seems that, in their play with drawn structures, children make free-flowing associations and multiple meanings. Perhaps this is the start of making puns. This is very important, because it could be the beginning of the child's ability to use rep-

Figure 84 Letter forms 'describe' what is happening in this drawing by Ben, aged three years and three months. Letter forms are also enclosed inside the closure to the right, representing people in a house. Notice the use of U shape on baseline for the wheels of the diesel engine as well as the upper-case letter (just behind the engine) perhaps meaning 'B' for 'Ben' and the lower-case 'b' inside the house – perhaps meaning 'b' for 'Ben'

Figure 85 Letter forms are mixed with pictorial images, by Ben, aged three years and four months

resentation to reflect on representation itself. This ability to think about thinking, referred to by psychologists as *metacognition*, develops with age but its roots may be in the fluid interchanges made possible by the plasticity of neuronal systems in the brain in infancy. This is one of the reasons why the

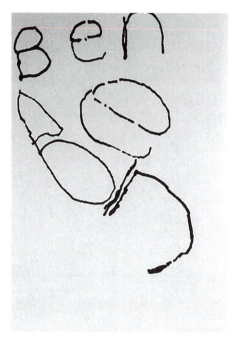

Figure 86   Linda writes Ben's name for him and Ben, aged three years and three months, 'copies' it

design of the learning environment is so crucial. Early childhood education has to allow such multiple associations and deep connections to be made. Unfortunately, much contemporary curriculum planning is designed with precisely the opposite intention in mind.

In Figure 85, letter forms are used almost interchangeably with more pictorial images and they really function as the visual architecture of this two-dimensional landscape. In Figure 86, Linda has written 'Ben' for him. Ben, aged three years and three months, has then copied these letters according to his own drawing schemas. These are dynamic patterns of action set into motion when a particular stimulus is encountered.

Most children are interested in the individual letter forms, but in their play with writing they also capture the linear, rhythmical flow of handwriting. Figures 87, 88 and 89 are drawn by Hannah, one after another, at age four years and ten months. In Figure 87, Hannah dictates to herself, 'Jamie and the magic torch ... Hannah and the magic torch ... Ben and the magic torch ...' carefully 'writing' these sounds as she speaks. Using variations of *travelling loop* and *travelling zigzag*, she is pretending to handwrite. Figure 88 shows a drawing she makes to illustrate her writing and which she clearly differentiates from it.

Figure 87   Hannah, aged four years and ten months, writes a story

Figure 88   Hannah, aged four years and ten months, goes on to illustrate her story

Figure 89   Hannah, aged four years and ten months; writing and drawing sometimes flow into each other

Figure 89 is important because it shows a mid-way stage, in which she partially draws and partially 'writes' the dark shape in the centre. The transcript of the tape recording reveals the way writing and drawing flow into each other. As she moves the pen she says to me, 'It's going round ... (as she draws rotational marks). It doesn't make sense ... what ... it ... makes ... is ... a ... little ... mess ... P ... P ... P ... for ... for Patrick ... (as she draws the looped form like a 'P' to the left). This looks like a swan ... because ... it is a swan ... ' (the writing action blends into a drawing action as she in-fills the shape with black ink). She is aware of the issues of 'making sense', of 'likeness' and 'non-likeness' in signs and symbols. Notice, too, that the structure of the vocalisations in time is reflected in the drawing-writing process. Like Ben, Hannah tests the limits of symbols and signs, building up an understanding of both differences and links between symbols and signs, and about their meaning, by allowing them to flow into each other.

Summary

Nancy Smith (1979) has argued that it is necessary for symbol formation that children, for a while, keep the way signs and symbols relate to the world rather amorphous. Children are aware of the differences between letters, numbers and pictures, but in order to thoroughly understand how they work, these shapes need to be incorporated into their play worlds. Here, they are taken apart and put together in different ways, which helps the child to understand how these shapes encode meaning. Because certain letters (those in their own names, or the names of their friends, or the names 'Mummy' and 'Daddy') are very significant to them, they become part of their own symbol systems. This means that children's drawing and early writing, though made up from identifiable (and to a limited extent, predictable) drawing rules, are unique, personal, visual languages. The way in which basic visual structures are combined together is unique to each individual. There are some important implications for teaching here. We should allow children to free-flow play with written and drawn characters (Ferreiro and Teberowsky, 1982). In work on literacy by such people as Marian Whitehead, Tina Bruce, Chris Athey, Vic Kelly and Geva Blenkin, there has been a shift of emphasis from the idea that reading is best taught as a series of visual and motor skills (recognising shapes, training hand movements and scanning lines of print, and so on) to the idea that it is to do with understanding and making meaning.

Of course, highly literate citizens are sometimes considered dangerous to controlling power groups and, unfortunately, during the last 15 to 20 years or so, there has been a tendency to reduce the idea of 'reading' to mere shape recognition and chanting of words. It is undeniable that some children do need special help in building words (Linda Matthews, 2002, personal communication). However in some 'National' curricula changes, the most central aspect of language use is in danger of being lost altogether, one of the most fundamental being the art of conversation (Linda Matthews, 2002, personal communication). If children cannot talk and listen they will certainly not learn to read. No amount of chanting your phonemes will alter that situation (Whitehead, 1990). To become literate, in the deepest sense of the term, very young children need to get their hands on real materials, have real conversations with real (not virtual) people. Only in this way, with the help of supportive adult companions, will children work out the meaning and use of semiotic systems.

Thomas and Silk (1990) have made the important suggestion that researchers of emergent writing should look more closely at how children draw. We all have to expand our notion of literacy and what it means to 'read' and 'write'. This expanded definition has to include all kinds of visual images – those made from physical paint, pens and pencils of all kinds and those produced electronically, for example, on a computer. It should also be sensitive to the ways in which different people 'read' and understand their personal worlds, in the sense that Paulo Freire means. It should not be restricted to elite classes or to the rich. Tragically, education has become more elitist than ever before. It seems that, once again, you need big money to be educated. Yet speech is fundamentally linked with class. As fewer and fewer of what Freire terms the 'popular classes' (Freire, 2000) enter into education, so there are fewer teachers with the necessary knowledge of different class groups, making a vicious circle – teachers who do not know that there is a problem, let alone try to find a solution for it. We should also be aware that children cannot just copy any letters or numbers. In writing, as in drawing, they start to notice and produce those shapes which they themselves have already started to produce on the drawing surface. This means that children take an active part in the construction of the visual environment of pictures, written language and numbers.

So far we have seen that children explore the relationships between lines, shapes and colours. In addition, they give powerful emotions to painting and drawing actions. They might notice that their moods affect the quality of the painting in different ways. They also start to realise that lines and shapes, and

8

Children begin to show depth in their drawings

By thinking about the different meanings suggested when lines and shapes are joined together in different ways, many children start to glimpse another representational possibility. Many children, as they mature, seem to want to show depth relationships in their drawings. We do not know if this is a natural, universal tendency or whether it occurs because of cultural influence. Some forms of art are not concerned with showing the third dimension at all. Islamic art does not represent any living thing, or the environment in which such things live, but uses mathematical patterns – the deep structures of representation. Where art has been concerned with representing the third dimension, the way in which this is done varies enormously from culture to culture, and from time to time.

But although art manifests itself in an infinite number of forms, some of its roots are universal and deep, and concerned with human issues and their representation. At the basis of many forms of art is a concern with the location of the shapes and movement of objects as a means to uncover their identity. Even religious Islamic art is about these issues, because it is based upon the concept of the 'point' and the 'moving point'. Perhaps the question of differentiating between nature and nurture in the world's art, is as meaningless as it is in human development.

To argue, as some have, that children's development in art is solely to do with the images they see around them and the expectation that their particular society has of their representational development, is an insufficient explanation. While some societies have an expectation that children should show the third dimension in their drawings, and some even try to coerce them into doing so, this is not a satisfactory explanation of an often-seen process of development. It is very important to understand that the steps children make towards this cannot be accounted for by the kinds of instruction or even coercion that they might receive. As children try to represent, they often come up with solutions which they would be unlikely to have encountered in their own societies or in their pictorial environment. They produce pictures which they would be unlikely to have seen in books or on walls. There is a strong tendency for children to try to add the third dimension as they draw and paint. However, this process is not explained by the classic story about a progression from non-representation to 'visual realism'.

The drawings Ben makes reflect the way in which he builds, as he grows older, an internal description of reality in which all its different aspects – height, width, depth, mass, weight, movement, plus the imagined psychological states of imaginary people in this world – are co-ordinated. This is eventually so fully worked out that he is able to imagine himself moving through it to any position and, from that position, imagine what the view would be like.

In this chapter we will consider how Ben co-ordinates these different aspects of his represented world. In some respects, Ben's drawing develops more fully than that of many other children. Drawing and painting formed a central part of his life. However, I am using this sequence because it clearly illustrates a path of development which has something in common with other children and because careful analysis of the sequence of steps, through which he moves, sheds light on how one might help other children's visual representation. For example, Ben starts off by encoding topological relationships, a kind of geometry which tracks movement in space. He describes paths of movement between positions in terms of both a continuous or broken line. He later defines spatial relations including inside and outside: boundary, closure and hollowness. Gradually, he starts to construct objects on the paper, not as simple closures, but with additional features with which to identify them. Further specifications can be added to simple shapes. For example, a closed shape can be made *long*, to show something long, or corners might be added to a closure to depict corners of a car or house. Ben, like most other children, also combines shapes together to show differentiation within forms, like the way legs are different from, but attached to, bodies. He also shows that some objects are above or below other objects. In this way, he maps onto the drawing surface a vertical axis. These steps are typical of most children.

Looking from a particular point of view, or a variety of points of view

What is less typical of other children, though not absent altogether, is Ben's realisation that shapes can suggest certain lines of sight or points of view. For example, he has realised that a closed shape can represent a 90 degree line of sight to an object (or 'face-on' view), and that a single line can represent a line of sight of zero degrees to a flat plane (or completely foreshortened view). This is a very important discovery, and we shall see how he develops it.

Eventually the understanding that drawing can suggest flat planes rotated through 90 degrees, is co-ordinated with the understanding of how movement of objects to and from a viewer can be represented on the flat paper. At first, Ben thought about successive points in space and time through which an object moves. This started with continuous lines or sequences of dots across the page, from one side to another. In Ben's case, these were gradually resolved into serialised images or 'picture stories' (also produced by other children) including kings falling off castles, boats taking off out of water. Note that these picture stories are unlike the comic strips in which sequences of movement are broken up into individual 'frames'. In Figure 90, Ben draws a pirate moving through a secret tunnel and then through the air, in a sequence of positions through time and space. We can interpret Ben's serial images in various ways: there is no fixed point of view; or there is a combination of multiple viewpoints; or another explanation is that no viewpoint at all is specified. Such drawings have something in common with certain Chinese paintings of figures shown at various positions of their journey, or

Figure 90   A pirate moves through a secret tunnel and flies out of the end, moving through five positions in space and time, by Ben, aged four years. Notice that the configuration representing the pirate changes size as it is repeated from left to right. It is drawn bigger in Position 2 and then drawn successively smaller until it is at its smallest in Position 5. Is he trying to show the pirate looming and receding in depth?

early Renaissance paintings in which an image is repeated within the same picture to show the same figure at different moments in space and time.

In addition to thinking about how a figure might move across a page, Ben gradually considers how an object recedes away from him or comes towards him. In doing so, he has two important new ideas. First, he thinks about how objects appear to get bigger as they loom towards him, and appear to diminish in size as they move away (something he has experienced since birth [see Bower, 1974, 1982]). This is called *optical* or *apparent size change*, meaning that the real object does not actually, physically expand or shrink but only appears to do so. A little of this effect can be seen in Figure 90. It might be that the initial size changes are at first accidental but then, as he realises the possibilities of changing the size of the drawn shape to show depth, he uses it intentionally as he continues the drawing. John Willats has called this behaviour 'the interaction between production and perception' (Willats, 1984, p. 111).

His second important idea is that, by thinking about this direction of travel, away from his own body or towards it, the relationship of an imaginary observer to the scene becomes important. It is as if someone is looking into the picture, as if through a window opening onto the scene. The edges of the paper are like the window frame. In other words, he is creating a single viewpoint. Through this window we can see objects *apparently* getting bigger or smaller, as they come towards us or move away from us respectively. Gradually, Ben is acquiring the freedom to move around his internal model of the world and study the scene from different positions. A similar change is reflected in the paintings of the Western Renaissance. Gradually, the painter became an individual, an independent agent, free to move through three dimensions of space and the dimension of time. Many art forms of the Eastern world too, show depth relations (although Asian art did not originally adopt a linear perspective solution).

Drawing a stagecoach that moves away from us

In Ben's drawing we can start to see the construction of a depth relationship when he is only three and a half years old (see Figure 91). A stagecoach moves along, not only from left to right but also away from us into the distance. He achieves this effect by making the repeated image of the stagecoach get smaller to represent the stagecoach moving away from someone watching it. He represents on paper how objects *appear* to get smaller, as they go away from us by his use of a controlled change in the *actual* size of the drawn

Figure 91   A stagecoach recedes into the distance, by Ben, aged three years and six months

image. Children understand that the size of most objects remains constant – they do not normally shrink. This might seem very obvious, yet in order to show, in a drawing, that an object is moving away, it is necessary to put severe constraints on the knowledge of the constant size of objects, to put it 'on hold', as it were. This means that Ben is forming a different attitude to the drawing surface. He is imagining that the paper is like a window opening onto a physical world. I write 'like', because in some extremely important respects, it is nothing like this at all. It means forming and co-ordinating a quite new set of drawing rules. To do this, Ben mostly uses the same kinds of shapes, lines and line junctions he has used before. The difference now, is that, what they represent in the real world is different. He is gradually changing their denotational values (Willats, 1997).

Figure 92   A steam engine, by Ben, aged three years and three months

One important example is the new representational values associated with oblique lines. We can see the glimmerings of this in Figure 91. If we place a ruler on the drawing so that it touches the top of each stagecoach we can see an implied oblique line. In later drawings this oblique line will become more explicit and the new way in which he uses the oblique line signals a revolution in drawing development.

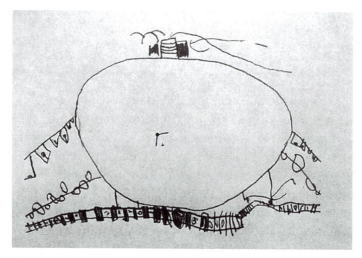

Figure 93   Multiple aspects of a steam engine, by Ben, aged four years and three months

In Figure 93, produced at the age of four years and three months, he shows us four views of a steam engine and its carriages. There is the front view of the engine; a plan view of the railway tracks; and a view of each side of the carriage. Such drawings have often been termed 'fold-out' drawings, but as Arnheim (1954, 1974) has pointed out, this is a misnomer, because nothing, for the child, was ever folded in, in the first place! This term, like others given to various kinds of children's drawing, reflect adults' – not children's – lack of understanding.

Drawing which combines two different sorts of knowledge about trains

On the one hand there is 'object-centred' knowledge which is about the main characteristics of objects irrespective of any particular viewpoint. That the carriage has two sides is an important part of this knowledge. However, Ben has also been influenced by 'viewer-centred' knowledge, which is about how things appear from a particular viewpoint. So, even though he has shown two sides of the carriage, which cannot be seen simultaneously in real life, each carriage side taken individually is like a view of the carriage. This is because of the new use to which he puts oblique, parallel lines. These lines represent the roof and floor of each carriage. The significance of this is that the slanting lines represent edges which, in reality, do not slant, but in fact remain horizontal. Within the context of this drawing, these sloping lines do not represent physical slopes; they show horizontal edges which recede away from the viewer of the picture.

The importance of understanding children's thinking

It is important to remind ourselves that Ben's development does not occur in a vacuum. There is a social context which includes interested and informed adults talking to Ben about how the drawings work, a ride on a real steam train and also other people's pictures of steam trains. Ben had been very interested in steam trains from the age of two years and ten months. He covers a toy engine in rolls of plasticine to represent the smoke coiling and wreathing around it. He is impressed by this unexpected behaviour of smoke, when we travel on the Isle of Man's steam railway. When the engine stands at the station, wreathes of smoke do not only travel upward but also coil and roil all around the bodywork of the engine. He plays at being a steam train, even insisting on 'shunting' backwards along pavements making 'choo-choo' sounds. Ben produces many drawings and avidly collects photographs and other pictures of steam engines. He also likes children's books about steam engines, including *Thomas the Tank Engine* (Awdry, 1997). Although his serialised images of steam trains are not like the comic books he looks at, the discussions with Linda and me about how these comic books work helps develop his ideas about how to show movement on paper and about the structure of events. This is also true of the way he uses other images available within his culture (Wilson, 1997a; 2000).

When Ben looked at photographs, they were, of course, in perspective, as were many of the pictures he collected. Yet Figure 93 is not in perspective and is unlike any of the pictures in his collection. Again, we have a glimpse of how his patterns of thinking, or schemas, allow him to organise his experience. He accepts and selects (or assimilates) some aspects from his collected pictures while rejecting other aspects. For instance, in some of his collected pictures, parallel, oblique lines represent receding horizontal edges of carriages. Ben has been able to assimilate these to his existing schemas. He has been able to accept the new idea that sloping lines do not necessarily mean slopes. He has learnt this by discussion and by analysing the two-dimensional structure of other people's pictures and photographs in his collection. Children visually analyse and use images found in the pictorial environment (Wilson, 2000) but this is not understood or recognised by the vast majority of advisers. One mistake is banning the use of ready-made, existing images ('second-hand' images, as these advisers call them). Another mistake, equally destructive, is to use the famous artworks as 'good' cultural canons or exemplars which children 'ought to know about' and emulate.

Ben has not been able to use other aspects of his collected pictures. In photographs of trains zooming towards him, oblique lines do not remain parallel but converge at the horizon at a vanishing point. When he draws perspective views of trains, Ben is not yet ready to use this convergence of top and floor of the carriage. Perhaps it conflicts with his object-centred knowledge that the floor and roof of the carriage must not touch.

Children's so-called drawing 'errors' are really sensible decisions about which information should be encoded in a drawing. Children's priorities about which information to keep and which to sacrifice changes with age and also depends on the context. At this time, Ben may want to preserve the parallel relationship between roof and ceiling. Other children resist showing depth when drawing objects like tables because this would sacrifice parallel edges and right-angled corners (see Figures 42 and 43 in Chapter 5).

It is worth reminding ourselves that, just because children may not use a certain drawing system, this does not mean that they cannot produce this system in other drawing contexts. Nor does it mean that children simply cannot make the types of lines required. Ben has been able to produce converging and parallel lines since the age of about two and a half years. His use of approximately parallel, oblique lines in Figure 93 is not explained in terms of motor-skills development but in terms of a conceptual, imaginative and intellectual leap. The revolution going on in his drawing is to do with the meanings of the lines, not the lines themselves (Willats, 1997).

Helping children get on with their drawings

The teaching implications here are that we need people who understand these drawing systems and who can talk to children intelligently about how these work. We need people who can identify the beginnings of these systems in children's work, possibly even pointing out to them the connections between these and the same systems used by adult artists. This may seem daunting, but in actual fact children do not always need much advice, although when it is given it does have to be of the helpful kind. They do much of the work themselves, as they try to resolve ambiguities in their drawings which they themselves find unsatisfactory or disturbing. As children draw, they receive visual feedback, and they then try to change the look of the drawing in response to this feedback, as can be seen in the following example.

In an earlier engine drawing (made at three years and three months) the wheels are placed upon the uppermost line of a plan-like view of a railway track (see Figure 92). (In fact, such plan views are soon modified, sometimes within the process of a drawing. In Figure 92, for example, he is starting to draw some of the 'sleepers' obliquely, as if suggesting that they recede back through the picture-plane).

A year later, Ben is still making decisions about how the wheels should fit with the railways tracks, and sorting out ideas about depth relationships. In Figure 93, for example, consider the relationships between the carriage sides and the tracks now. We will gradually see him resolve and co-ordinate these problems. Arnheim (1954, 1974), and Willats (in personal conversation), have argued that progress in drawing is unlikely to arise from the child being exhorted to somehow 'look more closely' at nature, but out of the child's looking at what emerges on the drawing surface itself. We can see this happening in Ben's next drawings. It is significant that Ben produces only one example of the so-called 'fold-out' drawing. This might be because he perceives in the finished drawing (and perhaps in the drawing procedure) certain ambiguities which he tries to resolve in subsequent drawings.

Over the following weeks we see him trying to sort out the potential conflict between information which tells us about the object in itself (as Piaget puts it), irrespective of any fixed viewpoint, and information which does specify a particular viewpoint to the scene. In Figure 94 we can see a steam engine moving towards us from the horizon. He has omitted the sides of the carriage in this drawing, perhaps in the spirit of tackling one problem at a time. This drawing is an important landmark in his control of grading size difference to show movement away from, or towards, an imaginary viewer. Compare it with the stagecoach drawing he did nine months before (see Figure 91). In his new drawing (Figure 94), we can see again the implied convergence between an imaginary line which connects the wheels and another imaginary line which connects chimneys.

Figure 94 A steam engine moves towards us. Ben, aged four years and three months, draws it in a series of positions as it moves through a continuum, from optical infinity *or the* horizon

Figure 95 A steam engine. The 'sloping line' on the drawing surface, representing the carriage roof, stands for what is, in reality, a horizontal edge receding from us. A drawing by Ben, aged four years and three months

Produced a week later, Figure 95 shows just one side of the carriage. An oblique line now means a horizontal edge which recedes from us, into a three-dimensional space imagined beyond the drawing surface. Up until one month before, a 'sloping' meant just that – a physical slope, that is, an oblique line in two dimensions (see Figure 96).

Figure 96 In other drawings, 'sloping' lines tend to represent physical slopes. This drawing by Ben, aged three years and eleven months, shows a rider on a giant horse which is reaching toward a man standing on a slope

Figure 97 A strange figure drawn by Ben aged four years and three months. Note the encircling belt

It is important to say that, in common with most children, and contrary to the assumptions of most drawing research, depth depiction is not the sole or most important concern in Ben's drawings during this period. He also produced quite fanciful drawings (see Figure 97).

In these, the devices he uses elsewhere to show depth, are used differently, they are decorative embellishments rather than lines and shapes which show volume (see Figures 98 and 99).

Figure 98   Figures with fish, by Ben, aged four years and three months

Showing the third dimension of depth is only one of an entire set of possible concerns children might have in drawing. It is not, as many people believe, the major end point of drawing development. For example, in Figure 98, Ben seems to be thinking of the figures in terms of arrangements of flat shapes balanced in ways only possible within this two-dimensional world. Even the three dimensions suggested by the folded tail fin of the fish are notional rather than realistic. Making a straight fold in a plane may be easier (generally) than showing a curved form on the two-dimensional surface (Willats, 1997; Matthews, 1999).

Figure 99   A strange sailor, by Ben, aged four years and three months

This strange seafaring man (Figure 99) has an interesting fez and spectacles. This sailor has a picture of a man on his shirt; a picture within a picture, as it were. Is Ben making a play of representation within representation? Also, notice the distant ship which, although drawn at decreased size compared with the foreground figure, nevertheless functions in a decorative or emblematic way, rather than as a device to show distance. Nor, in any case, did artists use linear perspective and other projective devices merely to show depth. They used drawing systems as much to show psychological transitions in time, or as a new way to tell a story in pictures.

Ben uses his new knowledge about how to show depth relations, but this knowledge is not stuck in any narrow system for producing so-called 'realistic pictures'. Rather, he combines a range of drawing devices to produce hypothetical universes. He also blends different genres (Wolf and Perry, 1988). Ben already knows that there are different styles of pictures, and what would be appropriate for one might not be for another. These drawings cannot be accounted for with that tired, old idea that children draw like this because they cannot do any 'better'! Very young children will show depth relationships sometimes, if those relationships are especially salient to them (Freeman and Cox, 1985; Willats, 1997; Matthews, 1999). Ben can do this if he chooses to. Children generally choose between a range of expressive and representational options. Their drawings are the result of reasons not causes. This has not usually been noticed, because the ways children do this do not fit into the definitions of most drawing research. Recently, computers taught to think topologically produce childlike drawings (Burton, 1997; Willats, 2002, personal communication).

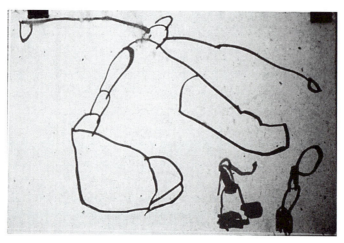

Figure 100   An extreme, low-angle view of a giant stepping over people, by Ben, aged four years and three months

Figure 100 shows a worm's eye view of a giant stepping over people. We have a very low-angle view of the giant, so close to his feet that they appear enormous, so far from his head that it appears tiny. Some people might object that the feet are big merely because Ben happens to be interested in feet; that these are drawn first, not allowing him much room for the rest of the figure. It is true that this can happen in many children's drawing, but it is not true of this particular drawing. Listening to Ben talking his way through this, and other drawings, confirms that he was trying to show depth. Another idea, that the larger the image drawn, the greater the emotional significance, may have been overemphasised. This idea has become part of the folklore of children's art, probably obscuring other drawing devices, especially the showing of depth relations. Nor is it true that the giant merely has disproportionately big feet. These are 'normal' giant's feet! They are drawn larger than any other part of him because they are closest to the viewer. There are even converging lines, perhaps the beginnings of true perspective, in the form of the giant's legs. Like other children, as Ben becomes interested in viewpoint he imagines himself moving, and imagines what the scene might look like from a variety of positions.

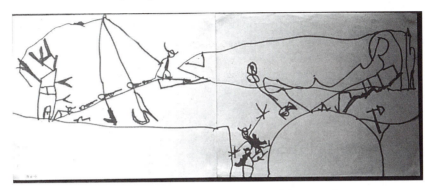

Figure 101 'A giant being crowned', by Ben, aged four years and three months

In another drawing, made a few days later, he shows the giant being crowned (Figure 101). We can see, to the right, a large, long, complex closed shape which represents the giant's crown. It is being carried by little helpers. As many of us know, when people carry large, cumbersome, heavy objects, there can be problems. In Ben's drawing, one of the carriers topples back, arms outstretched, into a hole, but is fortunately caught by a colleague. The story unfolds on the paper, sometimes his running commentary leading the drawing, sometimes the other way around.

The crown is to be carried along to the left side of the picture where it will be lifted up onto a series of platforms until it reaches the giant's head, a tiny closed shape, way, way up in the sky. Think about the relationship between crown and head. Ben is playing with the idea that, as the crown is moved towards the giant's head it will diminish in apparent size until it fits the head. Ben is playing with viewpoint and relative distances between the observer and different parts of the scene.

By the age of four years and four months he is making the nearer boots of soldiers pacing towards us larger than their further boots. Nine months later, a native North American indian is viewed from an extreme low angle. His leading moccasin looms hugely towards our eyes; so close we can see the decorations on its surface (see Figure 102). In another drawing made at four years and five months (see Figure 103), a horse, cowboys and native North American indians fighting, cowboys ascending a tricky summit, and a man hiding behind a wagon wheel are all drawn according to his criteria for realism. A study of the imagery on a 'Wagon Wheel' biscuit wrapper, for example, formed part of his careful research. But look at the sun. It is encircled with gun holsters and has a cowboy hat, complete with sheriff's star. When I questioned him about this he looked at me as if I was simple and explained, 'It's because it is in Cowboy Country!' This poses a question about what is 'realistic' for young children.

Figure 102   Extreme low-angle view of native North American indian, by Ben, aged five years and one month

Figure 103   'Cowboy country', by Ben, aged four years and five months

In his series of drawings about 'pirates fighting', we see many of his themes and understandings becoming co-ordinated. Look at Figure 104. Without a real knowledge of his intentions, and with naïve ideas of 'visual realism', many would judge these figures to be deformed and anatomically out of proportion; yet these shapes are the result of Ben's intense effort to imbue them with movement. He makes battle sounds as he draws. This is a development of those earlier associations between song and drawing action. In between bouts of drawing, Ben throws down his pen, stands up and, with his whole body, acts out the cutlass bout with an imaginary opponent. Then he sits down and continues drawing, perhaps now using interiorised imagery coupled with kinaesthetic information (about movement) and what is called 'proprioceptive' information (about the positions of his joints and limbs, about balance, posture and stress). Hence, the shapes on the drawing surface are not distortions of forms but attempts to give the drawing movement.

Dance, movement and touch are implicated here. Very young children sometimes move with grace. Those who are clumsy can be helped. Lise Eliot has pointed out the importance of physical contact – touch – between caregiver and child.

Touch is the closest way of showing care and love. We are probably never again handled with such intimacy as when we are babies. Greatest levels of communication occur when touch is linked with other sensory affective channels, included speech and gestures of the body. While in early years education we have a no-touch policy (mainly directed by women at male teachers), there can be no progress in this key area.

Vicktor Lowenfeld regards 'touch' as an important form of sensory knowledge which informs children's drawing. His idea of haptic information may overlap with the kind of knowledge traditionally called intellectually realistic. Haptic and kinaesthetic information is encoded in drawing from the dynamism of large body-parts, down to miniscule actions of the eyes. Look at the the man on the right in Figure 104, who is being struck by his opponent's sword. Ben is showing the knotted muscles around the eyes as the pirate screws up his brow in agony. This is a very unusual configuration for the eye region. Again, Ben acts this out, screwing up his eyes in simulated agony, opening his mouth wide, yelling. In the drawing, we can see his open mouth, the tongue showing. The man's eyes and mouth are drawn very differently from those of his opponent, whose eye is a dot and whose mouth smiles. He smiles because he is winning. In this way, Ben marks the difference between victor and vanquished. This is an example of how children's ways of drawing are not fixed, but vary according to what they are trying to do and the context of their drawings.

A child does not necessarily draw things in the same system. The function or use of an object, or the imagined states of mind of an imagined person will cause subtle or major changes in the construction of a child's drawing. It is vital that we appreciate this when evaluating children's drawing. Ben is differentiating between the two psychological states of the pirates. The depiction of the imagined thoughts and feelings of imagined people is just as important in drawing as showing depth and three-dimensional volumes. The intentions and motivations of other people are worked out in pretend play with imaginary people in imaginary worlds.

Like many of Ben's drawings at this time, this work is extraordinarily complex, using a wide range of understandings and influences. In addition to carrying powerful themes and content, this drawing is partially composed from a 'join-the-dots' procedure! Here, as elsewhere, we have a topologically based geometry. The topological understanding here is of how things connect. In this drawing, a line connects a series of points along a route. Young children are interested in this relationship and that is why 'join-the-dots' picture books are so successful with them. However, the use of topological geometry is not restricted to children. Mathematicians, electricians and computer engineers all use topology. The London Underground, Metro or MRT maps are based on topological geometry, as are diagrams of electrical circuits.

Figure 104 'Pirates fighting', by Ben, aged four years and six months

Occlusion and hidden line elimination

The pirates are superimposed over each other, but Ben soon finds another, powerful way in which lines and shapes can create space. He realises that it is not necessary to draw certain parts of a form if, from a particular view-point, these would be concealed from the viewer. That one can represent something by *not* drawing it is an important discovery in visual representation. Leaving something out, in order to show it, is not an achievement made all at once but through a series of investigations. The first step to representing occlusion is often to 'cover' or 'hide' a two-dimensional object by super-imposition. Paint is very good for this. A good example is when Joel (aged two years and eleven months) covers a blob of white with a second layer of green and says, 'The white is hiding'. In this example, the physical nature of paint conceals the preceding layer. However, a conceptual leap is made six days later, when Joel makes a larger closure around a smaller closure and says that the larger closure is a 'doggy' under which there is a 'baby' (or 'egg') (Matthews, 1984).

Figure 105   'Pirates fighting', by Ben, aged four years and six months

Unlike the painting of six days ago, the concept of an object 'hidden' 'under' another object, is here carried in Joel's imagination alone. In this drawing he does not have the physical nature of paint to actually cover and obscure a preceding layer, for he can see both closed shapes. Now, his description of over–under relations has been translated into line alone. Incidentally, this kind of visual description is misunderstood and misnamed by some psychologists who refer to it as an 'X-ray drawing'. They misinterpret its transparency as an error, instead of the conceptual achievement it really is.

In the drawings of pirates fighting (Figures 104, 105 and 106), we see Ben gradually leave out those lines representing forms which would be concealed by other forms nearer to the viewer.

In Figure 105, his second drawing, most of the shapes in the drawings are superimposed over each other, but at the bottom right we can see that Ben has left out those lines representing the part of the ship's mast concealed by the leg of the pirate. The concealing of one shape behind another in drawing is a special kind of overlap called *occlusion*. Leaving out the lines of the hidden or 'occluded' part is called *hidden line elimination*.

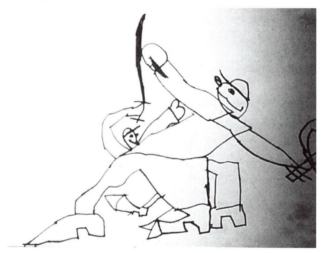

Figure 106 'Pirates fighting', by Ben, aged four years and six months

It is unusual for children of Ben's age to use these devices as part of an overall coherent system. Usually, they tend to draw uninterrupted boundaries of objects. Perhaps they feel it important to show the whole object as an entire, coherent form. This desire would be on a developmental route from their discovery in infancy of the shape, location and movement of objects, which together make up the identity of objects.

However, there are certain contexts, in which the very young will make use of a kind of 'proto-occlusion' and hidden line elimination. This happens when the boundary where one form passes beneath another is extremely salient to the child. One example is Figure 107. Drawings like this are often dismissed as 'stereotypes'. However, this is to miss the point that the right-angular junctions between leg lines and skirt line manage to suggest that the legs disappear behind, or under, the skirt. The child (a six-year-old Chinese Singaporean) feels able to use occlusion here because it does not disrupt the salient shapes of the legs (Chan and Matthews, 2002a).

Figure 107   A girl jumps from a tower building after a terrorist suicide aeroplane crashes into it. Human-figure drawings like this are often dismissed as 'stereotypes', yet, right-angular junctions between leg lines and skirt line suggest that parts of her upper legs are hidden or occluded by her skirt

Another example is Figure 42. For Campbell (aged four years and seven months), the boundary of the edge of a table is clearly very significant. He encodes this important information even though this entails sacrificing information about the lower parts of people.

In Figure 106, Ben's third drawing of pirates fighting, his understanding has reached a new level. There is no more superimposition. Ben uses hidden line elimination and occlusion throughout. When children discover a new language rule (for example, the use of the full stop), they often use it extensively, with great enthusiasm. In a similar way, Ben makes extensive use of these new drawing rules. The drawing is a dramatic arrangement of shapes, which overlap or occlude each other. There is an entire, undrawn body of one pirate hidden behind the other. His pointed, platform shoe is partially hidden by the other, its toe poking out of the other side. Ben is using what he knows about how things move; how a moving shoe disappears behind another shoe and, without breaking a continuous, smooth path of movement, reappears on the other side. Again, representation has its roots in the knowledge of dynamism.

Foreshortened planes

Earlier, we saw how Ben's drawings of 'beans on toast' and objects 'on top of tables', showed *foreshortened* views of flat planes. In Figure 106 we can see the hilt of the sword of the nearer pirate 'face-on'; that is, we have a line of sight of 90 degrees to its surface. The other pirate's sword hilt is shown completely foreshortened, or 'edge-on'. We can see how Ben's representation of depth has developed from the previous year.

Foreshortened and face-on views of an object representing two key moments in time

These are two opposite views. The child can only understand these different configurations as representing the same object when she has an understanding of sequences of events. These key moments in a sequence of action, when represented in images, tell us not only about the object itself but also about the object's past and future positions. Pictures which show how scenes look from a particular position in space show a moment in the flow of time. This is also true of the perspective pictures of the early Renaissance (Costall, 1992, personal communication). For children, showing three-dimensional looking scenes and depth in a picture is only part of the story. At deeper levels, this is the structure through which other ideas about the past and future states of affairs can be invoked. The greatest artists (children or adults) use perspective to show transition from one psychological state to another; the critical moment in an emotional relationship. Perspective is not just a way of showing depth but is the geometrical support or device for deeper levels of meaning.

The drawing surface as a 'window' opening onto a view

For some time now Ben has used the drawing surface as a 'window'. Now he has taken that viewer-centred approach a little bit further, to use this 'window' to show just part of the scene – like the viewfinder of a camera. The drawing surface is no longer a simple physical plane to support pigment but shows a selected sample of an imagined, bigger, visual array. This is a development of the concept of occlusion and hidden line elimination. In Figure

108, a soldier's face is so close to us that we can see the embossed pattern on his helmet and the scars on his face. The picture only shows his head; the rest of his body is 'cut off' by the bottom edge of the paper, (not quite the same as, but related to, the way, in which the girl's legs are 'cut-off' by the edge of the skirt in Figure 107). Unseen protagonists outside the frame, thrust swords into the picture. In fact we can see only a part of the entire battle suggested by the picture.

Figure 108   A scene of a battle, by Ben, aged four years and six months

This is unlike most other children's drawings made at the same age. Usually, children use the paper as a physical target, putting everything with its entire, unbroken form preserved, into the picture. In Ben's drawing, the edge of the paper itself occludes or hides massive sections of a scene which exist only in his imagination. Looking at the picture, we also need to use our imagination to fill in the gaps Ben has left. As adults, we are so used to this drawing convention that we are usually unaware of it.

Of course, this effect only works if all the elements within the picture obey the same rules. There is one part of Ben's picture which slightly contradicts this projective dimension. That is, the meaning of the line making the top edge of the embossed helmet. A distant figure runs up it as if it were a hill! However, even this ambiguity may be intentional. Even at four years and six months Ben may be making a game out of the rules of representation. A feature of children's play of importance to teachers and caregivers is that one can only play with rules when one has understood them. Ben does understand the drawing rules he is using. Such play with drawing rules is the forerunner of the more conscious use we find in later childhood and adolescence of using representation to reflect upon representation.

Planes, curves and spheres

At just over five years of age Ben produces a range of drawings in which spa-tial and temporal relations are further elaborated. In Figure 109, a knight in armour waves a sword at a knight on horseback. Look how he draws spheri-cal objects, such as the knight's helmet. By drawing the visor, he simultane-ously describes the helmet's curving surface. A belt encircles his waist in a now sophisticated use of occlusion and hidden-line elimination. This is also a development of the understanding of 'going round'. Look also at the dif-ference between the construction of this figure and the one on horseback. Although Ben is an unusual draughtsperson, most children vary their draw-ing construction according to context. The horse is interesting in this respect, being almost like a table in back-to-front perspective, with attached horse's head and mane. When children do not have much experience of a subject, they adapt their existing drawing schemas to the situation as best they can (Karmiloff-Smith, 1990).

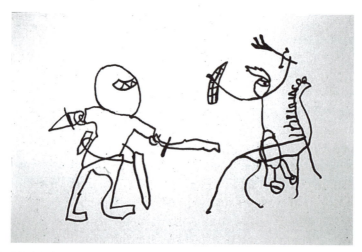

Figure 109   A knight in armour and a knight on horseback, by Ben, aged five years and one month

Direction of travel

Further evidence that time and space relations are involved in visual repre-sentation is shown in Figure 110 made by Ben at the age of five years and four months. The man is saying, 'Aha there pirates!' Because he is now at infants school, I tentatively suggest to him that the words and letters are back to front. He looks at me as if I am stupid and says, 'Don't be silly, the words

Figure 110 'Aha there pirates!', by Ben, aged five years and four months

come out of his mouth that way!' Even at this level, drawing and writing are still rooted in children's understanding of patterns and directions of movement. Essentially, the way the words travel from the man's mouth is based on the same understanding of the way a cannon ball comes out of a cannon's mouth (at the bottom left-hand corner of Figure 110).

From prehistoric times, language may come from using our hands, coordinating them in space and time to perform tasks. What we enacted with our hands was then imagined in an articulated form in our minds. The next step may have been the making of tools. Thus, the origin of language may reflect the structure of events as reflected in actions which were then reflected in the tools with which we extended our actions (Gibson and Ingold, 1995).

Again, a moment's further 'reflection' tells us the significance of children's drawing as a part of literacy.

From the age of six and a half, Ben produces a series of drawings based on his experience of 'Star Wars' movies (see Figures 111 to 116). It is interesting

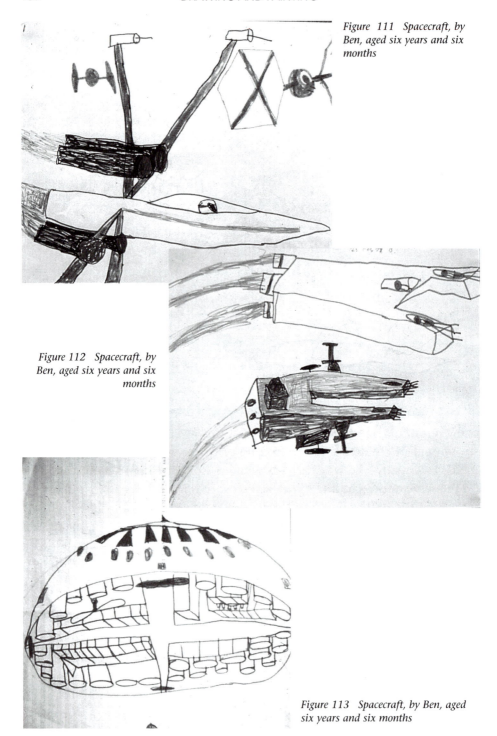

Figure 111 Spacecraft, by Ben, aged six years and six months

Figure 112 Spacecraft, by Ben, aged six years and six months

Figure 113 Spacecraft, by Ben, aged six years and six months

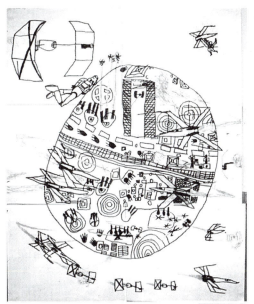

Figure 114   Spacecraft and artificial satellite ('Death Star'), by Ben, aged six years and eight months

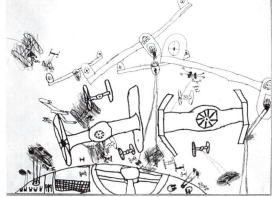

Figure 115   Spacecraft, by Ben, aged six years and eleven months

Figure 116   All Terrain Armoured Transport (AT-AT) by Ben, aged nine years and two months

to compare these drawings with the original images from the films. As we have seen right from the outset, other people's pictures only influence Ben's drawing to the extent that he is already drawing similar structures. His drawing of spacecraft is rather different from the originals because he filters these influences through his own internal schemas. We have seen this process again and again in development. It tells us something about appropriate teaching, what to suggest to children and what not to impose. Our provision of examples should be guided by careful study of how children organise their drawings. This does not mean that children can only draw what they already know how to draw, or should only be given subjects (or objects) which they can already draw. New suggested subject matter needs to be based on the children's drawing schemas, but could require them to adapt and revise existing drawing schemas, or to combine them in new ways. Actually, this tends to happen naturally. There is rarely an exact match between the subject matter to be drawn and drawing schema.

Nor can or should there be an exact match between what is shared in conversation between child and adult partners. This is the approach advocated by Vygotsky (1986) and others, in which the teacher is anticipating what the child is moving towards. This process is assisted by the children's spontaneous search of the visual environment for subjects which, although they fit to some extent existing drawing strategies, also demand revision and adaptation from the children. Vygotsky's ideas about this and the related idea of 'scaffolding' have been notoriously misinterpreted these days and distorted into yet another kind of interference of children's art and work, part of the general intolerance of what is perceived to be unsupervised or non-instructed activities. The iron hand of control is quite visible in most contemporary so-called educational 'reforms' in these New Dark Ages.

Ben intersperses drawings of spacecraft with other subjects, which nevertheless requires him to elaborate the ways in which he articulates forms in space. The drawing of skateboarders (see Figure 117) is one example. It is an unusual drawing for a child aged six years and ten months.

How has he achieved this? Does he have a complete picture in his mind which he somehow copies? This is almost certainly not the case. More likely, is that it is an interaction between his internal pictures and the shapes which appear in the drawing. Gradually, he has been able to generate, within his brain, a range of different views and to co-ordinate and manipulate these in different ways. When he draws, he modifies his internal actions of picturing according to the spatial relationships suggested by the shapes appearing on the paper. In a two-way process, his internal picturing guides his drawing and, reciprocally, what he draws – as it appears on the paper – helps his internal picture to develop. Drawing helps him rotate objects in his imagination.

Figure 117   Skateboarders, by Ben, aged six years and ten months

The skills of running internal pictures of scenes are part of the process of thinking and have links with mathematical, linguistic and logical understandings. How has he formed these skills? One activity which has helped his construction of thinking is that which we call *play*. He has created miniature worlds in play in which handheld *toys* including toy air and spacecraft, vehicles and people, are carefully moved through a range of orientations in three dimensions. In this play he adjusts his line of sight to the toys, seeing how they look from different positions (see Figure 118). Like other children, he discovers the technique of closing one eye to view the scene. He does this to cut out the variation between the images of two eyes and so obtain a single or *monocular* image. Although others insist that such practices are derived or imitated by the child from existing art practice (Wartofsky, 1980), observations show that this is not the case. Nor are Vygotsky's predictions that children are inducted into culture by copying adult routines and practices borne out.

My studies of British, Australian and South East Asian children show that they discover, through play, the strategy of obtaining a single image from a continuously rotating scene. This is a device which artists use in order to see three-dimensional scenes as single images from single viewpoints. Perspective drawing is based on this one-eyed vision of the world. Try it yourself:

close one eye and obtain a monocular image of the world. This is the basis of perspective pictures.

Figure 118 Six-year-old Chinese Singaporean children adust their lines-of-sight to obtain particular views of handheld toys, *'flown' in* play

A special kind of nothing

However, though spontaneously generated, this development requires support from understanding adults. A central part of this support is simply allowing this development to happen. Now, this point can be easily misunderstood. Undoubtedly Ben has inherited genetic predispositions and abilities from Linda and myself, but I do not believe that his achievements can be completely explained by this. In Ben's case, the environment, and by this I mean the psychological as well as physical environment, is critical for development. However, this support is an elusive, subtle thing. Sometimes, simple permission is all that is needed to promote creative thought. Although disdained by many art educators nowadays, the advice of our great pioneers of children's art (including thinkers as diverse as Rhoda Kellogg and Nancy Smith) is wise; sometimes, the best thing the teacher can do is nothing. However, although this may sound strange, this is a special kind of nothing, informed by a background of support which has become so infused with the way in which we, as teachers, think, see and plan, that, although we can articulate in conscious words if need be, in real-life teaching situations it no longer remains overt.

For behind Ben's spontaneous art is a background assisted by careful discussion and assistance from his parents, in which his play and representation has been recognised and supported or extended by suggestions in line with his intentions. The skills he has formed in the handling and viewing of objects are at least partially the result of a special kind of childcare. Most children can be helped to achieve these skills.

Visual jokes: the relationship between humour and intellect

At just over seven years, Ben draws a picture of a motorbike made completely out of bananas (see Figure 119). When, and only when, one has complete mastery of a representational language can one make visual jokes and amuse friends. Humorous acts, with drawing, with the body, with speech and writing, are intellectual achievements based upon competence in representation (see also Athey, 1977; Reddy, 1991).

Figure 119 'A motorbike made of bananas', by Ben, aged seven years

John Willats's work (1984; 1997) suggests that the way children represent depth in their drawings is a self-driven, internal process. My own work supports this idea. However, Willats has suggested that when it comes to linear perspective, this will not normally be discovered spontaneously, but requires teaching. If this is so, when and how this teaching should occur is a vital question. We have seen that children cannot be merely 'trained' in perspective. Indeed, teaching any of the projective systems should be guided by careful observation and identification of the type of projective system children are using. I have ample evidence to show that premature training in linear perspective has destructive effects on children. Unless they are ready to make this intellectual leap, they will be merely led into yet another cognitive cul-de-sac.

Other subjects of Ben's drawing include the Normandy rescues in the Second World War. Some of this drawing, produced at just over nine years of age was derived from the history books he was reading. However, the image on the back of one drawing (see Figure 120) shows a low-angle view of a dead soldier, lying at the edge of the sea and, as far as I know, was derived only indirectly from books and movies, but more decisively from his pondering of the consequences of war. Playing about war and fighting is not usually about violence but about, at one level, line of sight, trajectory and moment of impact, and, at a deeper level, justice, heroism and the management of power. Warplay is the most tragically misunderstoood aspect of early representation.

Figure 120 'Dead soldier', by Ben, aged nine years

Destruction, injury and death also have a funny side. If that sounds shocking, think about the jokes adults and children make about these subjects. Think about so many great works in literature, that of Samuel Beckett's work, for example. We have to find the funny side of mortality. 'Always look on the bright side of life (and death)' (Monty Python's 'Life of Brian' 1979). Figure 121 was produced at nine years and three months and shows a weary-looking robot who, after an exhausting climb up a vertical ladder, has reached the top – only to be blown up a moment later. We can predict this by looking at what befalls his colleague who precedes him. In this drawing he conveys past and future states.

Figure 121 Robots get blown up, by Ben, aged nine years and three months

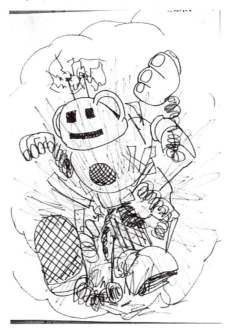

Figure 122 Robot exploding – close-up, by Ben, aged nine years and three months

The drawing made a little later (Figure 122) shows a close-up of an explosion. This change of view (or 'shot') is a cinematic effect. From the outset we have seen children coming to terms with the major fact of life that, in this world, things tend to fall apart. Drawings like this one are a continuation of these concerns in which humour takes the sting from disorder and death. It turns out that chaos may not be merely an unfortunate side effect of life, but the central generating force. Children's development in art is a superb demonstration of this dynamism.

Implications of Ben's development

The drawings depicted so far have focused on the first eight years of Ben's drawing ability. However, it is important to understand something of Ben's development in later childhood and adolescence, if the implications of the beginnings of drawings and paintings are to be fully appreciated. We have seen that drawing is a continuum of meaningful symbolisation which starts with the first drawing movements and marks. The ideas of Vygotsky, Piaget and Wolf suggest that this process is best understood as a conversation between the thinking child, his or her representational intention and the unfolding drawing (known as a dialectical relationship). Piaget thought that development was essentially a changing relationship between perception, cognition and representation. This transformation is reflected in the development of children's drawing. As Wolf (1989) suggests, the emphasis in this relationship changes as the child grows up. Whereas the younger child sorted out what the lines and marks stood for in the real world, the older child is more aware of further layers of meaning. The older child realises that a description of the surface content or structure of a picture may not in itself reveal the full meaning of an artwork. The older child is aware that there are hidden meanings. He or she is more in control of metaphor, that is, the use of lines and shapes to stand, not only for edges, boundaries and volumes in the world, but as ideas, feelings or themes for which there may be no literal description. This is not to say that these layers of meaning are not present in the work of a young child, for example, see Figure 123, 'Monster wind and power' by Chinese Singaporean, Darren, aged four years (Ma Ying and Leong, 2002). However, the older child may build upon these beginnings of metaphor and may gradually attain more conscious control of what Dennis Atkinson has called 'semiotic chains' of meaning (Atkinson, 2002 forthcoming).

Some of Ben's teenage drawings exemplify this. Figures 124 and 125 were produced at the age of fifteen. They were made after he was recovering from a brain tumour which nearly killed him. Figure 124 is called 'Rise and fall'. As in many of his drawings of this time, this work shows an individual in

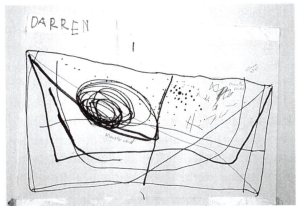

Figure 123   'Monster wind and power', by Bay Zhen Xuan, Darren, aged four years

Figure 124   'Rise and Fall', by Ben, aged fifteen

Figure 125   'Absorption', by Ben, aged fifteen

serious trouble. The man is falling, seriously injured. The outcome remains uncertain. He may rise again, we are not sure. Or he may rise again only to fall again – perhaps locked in a cycle of death and resurrection.

Figure 125 is entitled 'Absorption'. As in 'Rise and fall', the conscious use of double meaning in the title is more typical of the older child. Ben is depicted as an artist absorbed in thought. He is playing a game of life and death. Influenced by the work of the artist Escher, three-dimensional soldiers and a dragon arise out of the two-dimensional surface of his drawing (see Figure 126). They will experience a short period as three-dimensional beings before merging into the two-dimensional world again. Using ideas from 'Fantasy Role Playing Games', popular with teenagers at this time (and still popular, but often in digital form) the moves of the game of life and death are partly determined by a roll of a dice. We are not sure of the status of the game player. Is his life dependent on the roll of the dice? Or is he God, the Games Master, who can see eventualities, hidden from the rest of us? Or does God too, along with the rest of us, have to take his chances?

Figure 126 'Absorption' (detail), by Ben, aged fifteen

In both these works we can see a continuation of those themes which emerged in babyhood and infancy, when Ben thought about the beginning and ends of journeys. Now he is thinking about the beginning of life and its end, about where we come from and where we go.

How does the study of Ben compare with studies of average drawing development?

Statistical pictures of the average child's drawing have limited value unless we add to these detailed studies of individuals like Ben who use a representational medium intensely and develop at least some of its potentialities to the full. One problem with generalised 'stage' theories of development is that they assume a predetermined end point (whether this is 'visual realism' or some other expectation of children). Classic theories of development, including those of Piaget, Bruner and Vygotsky all tend to describe development in terms of the child gradually learning to overcome deficits in her thinking, and moving from the dynamic and physical to the ever more abstract, until the goal of 'correct' representation is achieved. As I have noted, a classical end point is visual realism but the nature of this realism changes from time to time and from place to place. What these different end states have in common is that they are forms of representation approved of and deemed correct by the society. The particular end point differs from culture to culture but it is always a preprogrammed series of stages towards being, in some way, 'good'. Stage theories also fail to show how the child moves from stage to stage. What are needed are more detailed studies of a few children which show the transition between one type of representation and the next. What is in between 'stages' is more important for study than the so-called stages themselves.

Autistic child artists

The general acceptance of a typical and generalised developmental route also leads to further confusion when unusually gifted children, including rare autistic child artists, are compared against this standard. Because Ben's abilities are not restricted to skilled drawing alone, but are highly developed in linguistic and mathematics skills too, his study is more useful to teachers and caregivers than studies of other exceptional draughtspersons who are supposed to have deficits in other parts of their reasoning. No one really knows why autistic children like Nadia and Stephen Wiltshire draw in the way they do. One idea is that because autistic children do not relate to the world and to people in the normal way, and are unable to play representationally, they may bypass representational problems which confront normal children. Because the world, for autistic children, does not hold the profusion of knowledge it does for most children, the idea is that it might be easier for them, than it is for ordinary children, to reduce it to a flat visual field. There are good reasons to disbelieve this theory (Costall, 1993; 1995; Seow and Matthews, 2000). Sometimes these unusual children are used to support a long-running fallacy about visual perception and representation. This idea is that the basis of human vision is a tiny 'retinal' picture formed in perfect perspective on the eye – rather like the image which passes through a camera lens. The basis of the story is that, autistic children, unburdened and 'uncorrupted' by meaningful relations and knowledge of the world, perceive and are able to represent the original perception, the original initial faithful image of reality, as if somehow copying it from the retina of the eye. Although many psychologists subscribe to this idea, it has no evidence to support it and is, almost certainly, nonsense.

A basic problem is that there are, in any case, very few artistically gifted autistic children. Another theory is that they are better able to translate visual images in their brains into the motor skills necessary to draw it on paper. This would make more sense in the light of what we know of the intimate relationship between action motor patterns and perception and language. It may be that, isolated islets escape devastation, go on developing and are driven by the self's desperate search to identify itself in relation to the world. Many autistic drawings are highly developed reiterative systems. It also seems likely, that the apparently meaningless actions of non-artist autistic children also are more organised into systems of representation, with the difference that the condition of autism confers these modes a denuded state. It may be that these children focus upon and build up reiterative systems, which are present in 'normal' children's drawing (see Seow and Matthews, 2000).

Along with the mythology of the autistic artist is another, equally contentious, notion. Most authors on autistic drawing claim that it is totally different from typical development. This is misleading because there are commonalities. When I observed Stephen Wiltshire drawing, he made excited sounds and movements in synchrony with his drawing actions, like the basis of representation we have studied in this book. It was hard to conclude that these actions were mimicry. Also, most accounts of autistic child artists argue that, because they cannot represent like other children, they miss out 'stages' of development through which most children pass. This also turns out to be untrue (Seow and Matthews, 2000). Given researchers' predilection for visual realism, the earliest drawings of these children were not collected. There is evidence that Nadia, for example, passed through a brief 'scribbling' period (Golomb, 1992) but this is rarely if ever, mentioned by writers about Nadia.

Other gifted child artists

Similar myths have been created about other gifted child artists not impaired by autism. Careful study reveals that they also seem to pass through a developmental sequence similar to most children. The Chinese girl, Wang Yani, for example, at age two and a half produced very beautiful rotational drawings and U shapes on baselines which, like many of the children in my own observations, she called 'mountain' and 'bridge'. Her first animal paintings at this time were composed of closed shapes with marks inside, and right-angular attachments. Of crucial importance is that her father appreciated these early visual structures and encouraged her (Zhensun and Low, 1991). Information about the beginnings of gifted children's drawing is usually skimmed over in favour of documenting the impressive artworks of their later years. This is a pity because such information would be very useful in what it might tell us about how these children extend universal strategies, and how this process might be supported by adults.

Studies of these children do not, as is sometimes claimed, throw all developmental theory of drawing into disarray. Explanations of autistic artists are muddled by a naïvety about drawing. Lorna Selfe (1977), for example, misleadingly terms Nadia's drawing 'photographically realistic' and she equates skilled drawing with deficits in other areas of cognition, thus perpetuating the myth that artists are unintelligent or strange. We need more careful studies of intellectually able children who are skilled in drawing to help dispel some of these myths of drawing development.

Summary

In this chapter we have looked at how children show depth in their drawings. Whether this is a universal, natural activity, or the product of cultural influence is a question which has no meaning in this theory. It is impossible to account for this development solely in terms of a simple imitation of cultural examples. This is because children often use pictorial devices they would not encounter in other pictures around them, and when they do incorporate strategies used in pictures they might see, they combine these in ways which reflect their internal processes of organisation, rather than the source pictures themselves. As they grow older, children may become sensitive to further levels of meaning. Whereas the younger child worked out what Willats (1985) terms the 'denotational values' of lines – what the lines stand for in the real world – the older child and adolescent may use images as metaphors for ideas, feelings and concepts (Wolf, 1989). This does not mean that this aspect is completely absent from the young child's representation. Indeed, early years teaching should provide for this possibility because this will influence the extent to which teenagers can consciously manipulate imagery to express ideas.

We also considered the relationship of Ben's drawing with studies of other unusual draughtspersons and painters. I suggested that, as with Ben's drawing, the development of the painting and drawing of these atypical children may share important features with that of more typical children. That this has not been generally acknowledged is due to the fact that those who write about these gifted children have failed to notice and understand the beginnings of the representational process in these artists' development.

9

Why do many children give up drawing and painting? What can we do to help?

Why do children give up painting and drawing when they draw with so much enthusiasm when they are very young? Our genetic inheritance certainly has strong effects, but we know that, even from the infant's intra-uterine experience, the environment and the opportunities it offers are crucial in the way the system develops (Eliot, 1999). Studies both of animals and babies show that development of the neuronal mapping of the system is triggered and stimulated by experience and practice. Self-initiated and self-directed movement are of prime importance. However, another crucial factor is the effect of other people. Other people also constitute a part of the environment. Babies interact with people in special ways which are launched to further levels of complexity with the acquisition of symbolic systems.

If we consider the example of children's drawing then we find straightaway that the contribution made by adults is crucial. We have seen that much of children's drawing and painting is self-initiated. It is fortunate that children keep their representational programmes running even in the face of hostility. Trevarthen (1988) has said that even though language acquisition requires other people, it does have a 'temporary autonomy' which will serve it for a little while if there is no support forthcoming from the environment. Derek Bickerton (1981) writes that language can be generated even if there is no adequate mother tongue available. He studied how babies created creole whose mothers did not speak this language, but only 'pidgin'. This strongly supports the theory that the process of language acquisition is initiated by structures already present in the central nervous system at, or near, birth. However, it would be a mistake to conclude that development in drawing, in language or in anything else is predetermined by a kind of little blueprint in the brain. For both language and drawing to fully develop, interaction with another language user is essential. Babies need an adult companion to share in the representational adventure in which meanings are given to sounds, actions and images.

In this developmental landscape there are many crossroads at which children must choose a direction. Although, children sometimes appear to get stuck in apparent impasses, these hold-ups need not be permanent. Although children may not always be able directly to tell you in words what they need, the language about their thinking will be present in their action, play and media use. The caregiver needs to be able to understand this language. Even the actions of a disturbed child will have their own kind of logic, which will contain a message about the nature of the problem (Bettelheim, 1987; Winnicott, 1971).

Using the patterns of development described in this book, it is possible for the caregiver to anticipate, and to a limited extent predict, what the child might be moving towards. There are times when children might seem frustrated because they cannot find a way to represent their new understandings about the world. At such times, they may be actively searching the environment for help. Sometimes they are looking around in the culture (in photographs and drawings, in books and comics, on television and in movies) for a particular type of image which will help them. Children can learn about the drawing rules which translate a three-dimensional world onto a two-dimensional surface. This is why it is so wrong to ban working from other people's pictures, as if these were 'second-hand' images. To think of this as mere 'copying' is to misunderstand development altogether.

It is at such crossroads that 'more experienced learners' can be involved, making suggestions or putting certain experiences in children's paths. This is the real meaning of Vygtosky's ZPD and scaffolding – not the current hijacking and exploitation of children's play towards a goal already deemed the most important by an adult. One example of this is when children become interested in rotating. In these instances, the caregiver might introduce a variety of interesting rotational experiences, from spinning tops to washing machines, and the nursery rhymes which are about rotating, like 'Ring o' Roses'.

Some people might think that children rotate because they hear these songs and copy them. Actually, it is the other way around. Children's schemas for rotation, both dynamic and configurative, cause them to choose these songs in preference to others. Hence these songs may have remained popular because of the demand created for them by children. I have used rotational songs as an example, but the same principle applies to other popular songs, rhymes, movies, and computer and video games. Children's choices from the pictorial culture give a good clue to possible learning experiences and materials. 'Jack and Jill go up the Hill' and 'Humpty Dumpty' are good examples of ascent and descent, as is 'I'm the King of the Castle', which Ben liked at the time he was drawing the king and the castle. The television programme *Teletubbies* is very popular with babies and young infants precisely because its script is concerned with basic relations and causal chains which interest them; emergent concepts of going inside from outside, going outside from inside, going up, going down, going through, going from A to B and back again. *Tom and Jerry* and similar cartoons have been heavily criticised by feminists who see in them machismo propaganda and male violence. This is wrong. Such animated 'cartoons' (from the Renaissance term meaning a preparatory drawing) are superb examples of trajectory and moment of impact. The animated-cartoon *CatDog* is a superb example. Cat-Dog is an animal with a Cat's head at one end of its body and a Dog's head at the other. This children's show also shows the causal relationships within events (often misinterpreted as male violence) plus it ponders additional problems about self-identity, resolution of emotional conflict and how to go to the toilet. In these brilliant movies the solutions to these problems are often found through camaraderie and the need to work things out together.

It is most unfortunate that this kind of material is sometimes not available to children in the school context due to mistaken ideas about moral guidance. Similarly, it is sad that other trajectory-and-impact games of both boys and girls, including pretend shooting games, have been misconstrued as macho violence and banned from many nurseries. The female-dominated, early years workforce tragically misinterprets the gunplay of young boys as a manifestation of male hegemony and violence. Early years educators should consider carefully, in a non-partisan manner, this criticism. Until this mistake is rectified, there is little point in sending one's child – male or female – to nursery or early childhood centres.

Children's development in symbolisation moves from level to level, making new layers of meaning like a palimpsest which freely flows in an interactive dialogue with the environment, and the experiences and opportunities the environment affords. Sensorimotor patterns become the structure for further layers of meaning. To use one example, children produce all manner of lines and line junctions, but their denotational values and representational values are shifted to new levels by changes in intellectual development. Consider one simple example, the sloping or oblique line. At first, this has directional meaning, sometimes made in reference to the real world. Later, it may represent a physical slope, inscribing an oblique axis or incline on the drawing surface. Later, however, the sloping line need not necessarily mean a physical slope at all, but a horizontal edge appearing to recede away from a notional viewer. This happens when the child nests this line within the beginnings of a completely new system which maps depth relations, or the third dimension onto the two-dimensional drawing surface.

When children start to use the oblique line to show depth, it might be relevant to discuss with them how these lines work, and to show them good examples of the use of oblique lines in other people's pictures. Most important of all, if we want children to continue to value art processes, then we, as adults, have to genuinely enjoy them. Children will differentiate between sincere responses to their own work and insincere ones. It is a question of establishing an environment in which permission and trust are given to children to explore their own representational landscapes. This is the kind of environment in which the different ways in which children and adults express themselves are respected, where children feel confident that people will take their drawings seriously, and where it would be unheard of for a child's drawing to be dismissed as mere scribbling.

It is never too early to discuss with children how their images work; it is just that one has to vary one's use of words according to the child's age. In babyhood, it is a question of participating in that four-dimensional language of gesture, facial expression and sound in the shared space and time between baby and caregiver. The language of this ongoing conversation gradually takes different forms as the child grows. The number of words you say to children is not important. Some children need to be saturated in ideas but it is not always necessary, or advisable, to say anything at all. As Nancy Smith has said to me, sometimes one has to tiptoe unnoticed by a child who is drawing. Tina Bruce (1991) has also made the important point that when children show you a drawing they may just want to share this with you and may not expect any criticism at all. It must be a shock to discover that your drawing, which you did for pleasure and which you wanted to share with an adult, is greeted with criticism. This behaviour on the part of the adult is not only a case of 'looking a gift-horse in the teeth' – it stunts development by amputating, at one stroke, one of its important limbs.

The main point is that you try to understand what the child is trying to do. From playing and working with young children I have found that they are often surprised and delighted that adults have serious terms for the drawings they produce. It is fascinating to them when (at last!) a grown-up has an intelligent conversation with them about their drawing. When we talk to them about how lines, shapes and colours are working, we are helping their language and mathematical understanding. We are helping them to articulate and bring to consciousness important understandings about how representation works. In doing this, children gain more awareness of the limitations and possibilities of drawing processes, and start to realise that some, but not all, of their representational intentions communicate to other people, and they start to understand the reasons for this. One is expanding a shared field of discourse and understanding. They start to learn the terms too. I had a three-year-old running up to me exclaiming, 'Dr Matthews! Dr Matthews! I've drawn a closed-sheep!' (closed shape).

Did my children see me painting?

Most of the time we protected Ben, Joel and Hannah from the worst excesses of my serious painting habit, but it is true that through the period of their childhoods I was really involved in my painting, and I believe this affected them. I did allow them planned glimpses of some of my working procedures but only those approaches which might approximately fit in with some of the understandings they were forming in their own painting and drawings. I have a feeling that exposure to certain types of adult painting might not be so helpful to very young children. However, it just so happened that the kind of painting which interested me at the time was concerned with very basic relationships between movement and image and I think that this approximately matched the concerns of my children. In turn my own painting and drawing was influenced by theirs, so it was hard to say who influenced whom – it was a two-way process. (In fact, this continues to be the case today – I am very influenced by the grown-up art of my children: Hannah's photography of women, Ben's performance art and Joel's rock music.)

But then, all the things that the children saw Linda and I do were in the context of an intimate relationship, that was part of an ongoing and seamless interrelationship, not focused on any end product. How could it be? Transactions with the family, involving electronic and traditional media, all manner of day-to-day handiwork, fixing broken things, basic carpentry, manipulating all kinds of things, form a background against which the child's expression and representation are formed. Most of this seems sadly to have been forgotten. An acquired universal amnesia encouraged by power-groups ensures that there is little tolerance for individual creativity, and builds systems to train people, once again, 'to know their place' (Ranson,

1984, p. 241; Simon, 1988, p. 43; Berliner and Biddle, 1995).

Should one paint or draw for children?

I did not draw for the nursery children. I did very occasionally draw for my own children, but usually in a minimal way, and based on what they could produce themselves. When I did draw for them, I explained as clearly as I could, what I was doing. I explained that certain effects were the result of the drawing rules, and helped the children understand the structure and content of their drawings. I also made my sequence of drawing movements easy to follow. Generally, Linda and I conveyed to the children ease and confidence and familiarity with materials and media, whether using cheap or waste materials or electronic devices. We did not worry about mistakes. My experience is that children, with a little supervision will be able to manage expensive cameras and other machines. In my work with John Jessel, I was impressed with John's approach to children's use of computers. Being, at that time, relatively technologically illiterate, I regarded computers as expensive, pristine, awe-inspiring things which needed to be kept sparkling new. John thought that it would be a good idea to allow the children to grubby them with paint and dirt! We taught them no rules except those of safety, that of the equipment and that of their own persons. With cameras, don't drop them! Keep the strap around your neck. Don't poke the lens because that's like poking it in the eye! Water and computers don't mix! If this sounds radical, do not forget that not so long ago children were not allowed to touch such technological marvels as pencil and paper.

However, after a quarter of a century of being involved with young children, I would still advocate that one draws for children with extreme caution. Because the majority of people are speakers, they tend to converse, even with the babbler, in ways which are better than the ways in which they interact with the scribbler. It is important to stress that showing my drawing and working process to children were small elements in a larger approach to childcare. Responding to and talking about their own paintings and drawings had a far more significant effect on the children.

The importance of record-keeping

Keep a record of the paintings, drawings and constructions children make. The paintings and drawings themselves form a good record of development.

But do not forget that it is not just the 'finished works' which are important. Much of children's action will have expressive and representational value and meaning. Look for the meaning behind all their actions. This will be a useful diagnostic tool for those children with behavioural (so-called) problems, disruptive, difficult or unsociable learning difficulties. Video recording is relatively inexpensive and very useful, and the children can record their own work with help. As I mentioned above, Rebecca Chan and I got two- and three-year-olds using video cameras. Try to see the same or related themes in different media, and in their play and speech. Conversely, try to see how the application of a familiar action to a different medium or tool, creates new and subtle variations. Do not take the work away from children too soon. Let them see it on show for an extended period of time, or help them to store it so that they see that they are building up a collection and that they can see their own progress. Ben, Joel and Hannah were given a variety of inexpensive drawing books of different sizes and quality which were always available for them to look through and to which they could return. Exhibit it well but try not to disturb the original quality and characteristics of the work. Do not merely 'tidy-up'. Do not chop up drawings with scissors and pinking shears. There is no space 'wasted' in a children's drawing. Cutting around the lines of a drawing destroys the child's sensitivity to the line. Give children an opportunity to display their own work. (I received this tip from early childhood educator, Judy Cooper.)

Nowadays, electronic paint can be projected directly onto a large surface, so that the child has the experience of accelerated painting strokes made in light and at incredible speeds which would have amazed painters like Jackson Pollock or Willem De Kooning. At a recent children's art exhibition, Jane Leong, Sylvia Chong and I had young children interacting with large-scale electronic paint, alongside more traditional forms (Ma Ying and Leong, 2002). Do not forget other forms of electronic media. Do not forget the performative aspects of children's expression; how might this best be represented and displayed? As a rough rule of thumb, everything that very young children do, unless proven otherwise, is art. Think about it.

Do not restrict painting to easels but use tables and floor too. Each has its own opportunities, advantages and limitations. Painting at an easel is valuable because one is in control of space, moving closer or further as you please, to and from your drawing or painting. You can preserve some of your own independence at the easel. On the other hand, easel painting is sometimes an isolated activity. Working at an easel requires particular skills. Standing and holding a brush against a near vertical surface can be exhausting. So use tables and chairs too. A group of tables placed together, with chairs around them means that children can talk to each other about their drawings, sit back and rest or view their own or others' work.

Intriguing and important interaction often takes place when children are allowed to paint and draw in this way. Children are often good teachers and this sort of interaction provides different learning opportunities from the limited kind allowed by easel painting. However, each arrangement, whether easel, tabletop, computer, is not simply 'good' or 'bad' but shapes the activity in certain ways. At an easel, for example, paint drips and runs, which can be an advantage or disadvantage. Painting at an easel can involve one's whole body, which might not be the case when painting at a table or a computer.

With traditional, physical pigments, there is a limit, in a busy classroom, to the number of colours one uses. With electronic paint, there is no limit about the number of colours which a three-year-old might use (Matthews and Jessel, 1993a; 1993b). This flatly contradicts the traditional theory that, only as they grow older, will children be able to use a wide range of colours. The physical and practical problems (for children and teachers), associated with preparing, distributing, and tidying away physical pigment, vanish with electronic paint. However, do not use this as an excuse to replace physical art materials with digital and electronic ones! There is no substitute for these traditional, physical materials. The point being made here is that development is context and medium specific. Claire Golomb also notes this in her studies of children's use of clay (Golomb, 1974; 1992; 1993).

Help children so that they can mix their own paints and display their own work. Of course, do not force anyone to paint or draw. If the ambience is right, the painting tables and easels will be inundated with customers. Nancy Smith has some good, practical ideas about layout for painting for the very young (Smith, 1983). The main thing is to develop sensitivity and a genuine interest in drawing itself; to its developmental patterns in childhood. Also, do not be rigid in your definitions; be open to the many forms of drawing. For example, does drawing necessarily have to leave a mark? Look at contemporary approaches to drawing (Rose, 1992; Rush, 1999; Button and Esche, 2000). Some postmodern artists use movement as a form of drawing, and there is certainly a link between drawing and dance (Davies, 2003). Drawing does not even need to be done on earth. Weightless painting has been produced in space (Pietronigro, 2000). I have also worked in Zero G, writing and drawing my underwater book (see Matthews, 2003).

Painting: the unfolding event

I would like to finish this chapter with a final observation of Hannah, at two years and two months of age, painting alongside Linda. Hannah is at the phase of development in which she is starting to produce closed shapes and dots. The following observation is taken from a transcription of a video recording which, for analysis, was slowed down to quarter speed. I have chosen this example because it demonstrates all the main principles of interaction and provision we have considered throughout the book. These principles remain basically unchanged regardless of the age of the child.

Hannah is drawing with brush and paint. She is standing on a chair at a table on which rests an A1 size piece of paper, some brushes and six pots of paint – black, red, yellow, purple, green and blue. Linda is seated at Hannah's left, within touching distance.

The sequence opens with Linda discreetly tucking Hannah's dress out of what she anticipates is Hannah's field of vision and movement. Hannah is attempting to lift a brush out of its pot. The brush is stuck and makes a squelching sound in the viscous paint. Linda's hands move in to assist, but it is only necessary for them to hover in readiness at the lip of the pot, for when Hannah lowers the red pot to the table the paintbrush is dislodged.

Hannah presses the brush against the paper. Then she raises it 15 centimetres and pauses for a fraction of a second. While Linda's hands remain on the red pot to hold it steady, Hannah again presses the brush down vertically and firmly against the paper. She hunches her shoulders, putting weight and pressure upon the point of contact between bristles and paper. Linda is opening her mouth in interest and surprise and, with the merest movement of her eyes, looking up to Hannah's face and back down again to the painting, focusing on the events taking place where the brush hits the paper. As Hannah presses the brush down, she slightly screws up her eyes, and through compressed lips, emits a 'raspberry' sound which lasts less than a second and continues as the brush is raised about 15 centimetres above the surface of the paper.

About 15 seconds have elapsed as Hannah stabs the brush down vigorously to the same point, synchronising a raspberry sound to the moment of impact. As she raises the brush about 15 centimetres above the surface she looks towards Linda, who returns her glance. This was impact number three. Then she makes a series of rhythmical stabbing actions with each impact in one-to-one correspondence with a raspberry sound. She increases the volume of the synchronised raspberry sounds. As she raises the brush she takes an indrawn breath, like a little sigh.

During impact number 5 (again synchronised with a raspberry sound) which occurs at a site a few centimetres further away from her, Linda's open mouth transforms into a smile which develops as Hannah stubs the brush down for the sixth time.

After the eighth stab, she makes a longer pause, looking at Linda who smiles at her. Then Hannah immediately returns her gaze back to the painting. She then makes a series of vertical arcs with the brush, gradually quickening the tempo. At the start, she holds her breath, but then gradually releases it in an audible sigh, breathing out as she increases the pace. She no longer synchronises vocals as she gradually rotates from the hips and shoulders making a series of spots in a wide arc around to her left and back again. This last impact is changed into a pull stroke which she visually tracks with an inclination of her head.

This seems to give her a new idea. She stops and pauses. She aims the brush in the direction of the red pot but suddenly appears to reconsider this. She has changed her mind. She drops the brush and moves her left hand towards a lid. In slow motion, one can see her fingers splay out in anticipation of the circular shape. It is at this moment that Linda's hands move in to assist, and in slow motion there occurs a beautiful ballet of interchanging hand movements between adult and child which centre around the paint pot. Linda 'scaffolds' the task (Gray, 1978, p. 169) but only to the extent that this enables Hannah to take the lead. Hannah presses down on the lid, but Linda discreetly completes the action of securing it on the top of the pot.

Hannah leans over to retrieve the blue pot with her right hand. Again her fingers splay out in anticipation of the form of the pot. She picks up the pot and successfully pulls off the lid with her left hand. Linda asks: 'What colour is that?' 'Bu', (blue) answers Hannah. As she puts down the blue pot near the centre of the paper, Linda reaches over the painting and removes the lid from Hannah's field of view and action. As soon as she has done this, she withdraws from the field of action and resumes her position at the side of the table.

Hannah is not aware of Linda's help for Linda seems to have timed this assistance to coincide with Hannah's preoccupation with her brush. In slow motion there is a beautiful ballet of hands and fingers as Hannah exchanges hand grips on the brush till she is satisfied that she has the best grip for her intended task. Her next actions are planned in advance. The dawning of this plan happened when she made the first trailing, rather than stabbing, motion of the brush. Now, she traces with the brush an anti-clockwise course around the blue pot which serves as an axis. As she draws this line she visually tracks its movements with an absorbed expression. With her voice she starts to make a 'shhhhhhh'ing sound which is synchronised to the slow-moving brush as she drags it around the pot. She looks up at Linda for appreciation as she corrects the flight path of the skidding brush. It flies off the paper and swings back against the edge of the table with a loud bang. They both pause for a moment to regard this point.

Hannah looks towards Linda who returns her glance. Hannah makes one more downward stab which seems to serve as a full stop, or even an exclamation mark, for the entire sequence. Then she stands, open-mouthed, panning her head from side to side, surveying the entire scene. Then she looks up to me and compresses her lips in a slight smile. 'That's amazing, Hannah,' I say. There is pause of about two seconds, while the three of us look at the painting, a blue, curving line partially embracing clusters of red spots. Then Hannah looks for the lid of the blue pot. Linda helps her replace the lid. Hannah retrieves the red pot. A new painting sequence is about to begin.

Analysis

A two-year-old starts and controls a painting as it develops

Careful analysis of the video recording shows Hannah making skilled drawing actions. Hannah is initiating and controlling complex, unfolding patterns of action in which actions of the limbs, facial expression, her breathing, speech, object manipulation, tool-use and appearing image are seamlessly co-ordinated for the purpose of expression. It reveals Hannah's understandings of objects and forces; about the relations between her own actions and the images these produce. It shows how Hannah is noticing and using expressive qualities of movements and their images.

Interaction between adult and child

In addition, the sequence reveals the complex levels of interaction between Hannah and her mother. It shows how an adult can respond to and support children's early painting. This single observation can serve to point the way to important general principles of interaction and provision. With Linda gently and sensitively supporting the lead taken by Hannah, they participate in a web of shared understandings and anticipations about what is unfolding on the paper's surface.

This is an excellent example of adult support for, and 'scaffolding' of, a child's task. Yet Hannah's mother, Linda, appears to be doing almost nothing. What she does do, however, is crucially important for Hannah's development.

Inside the envelope of space between adult and child

A mark-making event like this is a development of those exquisitely orchestrated interchanges between mother and child which involve movements of the body, face and vocalisations (Stern, 1977; Trevarthen, 1975; 1980; 1984; 1988; 1995).

Here we see rhythmical patterns of movement of each partner coupled together precisely. This allows Hannah and Linda to enter into deep states of empathy with each other. Trevarthen has suggested that there is a biologically standardised time-base for these patterns of actions against which we evaluate the significance of any variation in tempo, amplitude, cadence, accentuation or stress. When Hannah makes controlled variations in this timing she does so to create expressive and humorous effects.

Mother and child as companions on an intellectual adventure

Both infant and mother are sharing a field of view which is also a field of action. This consists not only of the physical surface of the paper, the pots of paint and brushes, but is also a window opening onto a variety of potential but unknown futures. They are both predicting and anticipating events which may occur at the surface of the paper. They are stepping together into the unknown.

Both child and mother know something of each other's viewpoint. When either makes a movement, the viewpoint of the other is taken into consideration. Consider the kind and quality of the mother's support for her child's behaviour. Linda's presence is crucial for supporting the child's task yet she barely moves! It is also notable that few words are spoken. Most of the communication between them consists of exchanged glances. There are different types of glance. Both parent and child seem able effortlessly to distinguish these. There is, for example, a questioning glance made by Hannah to which Linda frequently responds with an action instead of a word.

How Linda helps Hannah

There are many levels of teaching here, ranging from one of simple instruction (as when Linda asks, 'What colour is that?' and Hannah answers,

'Bu') to one of demonstration, and to much more subtle communications and shared understandings. The mother, mainly by her body language, gives a 'commentary' on the event (Harris, 1989, p. 22). Much recent curriculum design in Britain and elsewhere only acknowledges the instructional level, which is the least important level. The deepest level, really is the progenitor of representation, language and literacy. We need more studies about the interpersonal gestural and expressive language formed between adult and child, for it is part of the principles of teaching interaction. This should not be understood to mean that we can teach people how to do this in a fixed rigid sense, any more than one can 'teach' mothers how to play with their babies. Rather, it suggests that a completely different concept of the teacher–learner relationship be identified and developed (Blenkin and Kelly, 1996).

Linda is aware of Hannah's field of view and movement, entering this space only when absolutely necessary and in an unobtrusive way, her actions of management timed to coincide with Hannah's preoccupation with a brush or a pot. Linda withdraws from this space quickly, allowing Hannah to resume command of the movement. Linda only helps when a task (such as taking a lid from a pot) might interrupt the flow of Hannah's thinking, and then she moves her hands in a clear, defined way, respecting Hannah's field of view. In this way, the child is allowed to see what is happening and is able to take control again. At times, this scaffolding allows Hannah the illusion of complete mastery and control. It is not simply that this scaffolding creates an illusion in Hannah that she is in complete control, rather, the construction through time is negotiated between the dyad, that is, the 'tasks' involved cannot be separated out and studied in isolation from the relationship between partners.

Drawing is not a problem-solving situation

Both mother's and child's responses to unforeseen events are illuminating. Every response seems positive, whether it be one of surprise, humour or wonder. For example, when the brush flies away from the paper and bangs the side of the table, neither person is upset. On the contrary, they regard this event with the greatest interest. Some researchers habitually regard drawing as a problem-solving situation; this is incorrect and misleading. There are no problems here, although problems are ceaselessly being posed by the child. In good education children love problems; in bad education they fear them. There is interplay between the child's intentions and the chance occurrences which affect these. While Hannah continuously monitors and corrects the flight of the brush, she does so without a fixed goal in mind, but tolerates a wide range of variation from her initial plans. This is unlike the High/Scope method of early childhood education (1979) in which nursery age children are expected to plan in advance what they intend to do with play materials (Hohmann, Banet and Weikart, 1979). This runs counter to everything we understand about child development for it requires very young children to think at an abstract level before they have had the experiences of dynamic play and exploration from which abstract thinking grows. Nor does my theory fit into any National Curriculum plan, which always presupposes a predestined goal or 'correct' end point against which the child's actions are measured (Atkinson, 2002 forthcoming).

Hannah takes advantage of accidents, but not merely at the level of spotting chance resemblance, rather, a small sequence of movements (as when a stabbing motion is changed to a trailing one) suggests to her possibilities of new sequences of action which have embedded within them complex body movements from eye gaze to muscular and skeletal frame postural movement (Matthews, 1999).

Hannah makes the decisions

Linda's response to the fluid variety of this painting event is crucial. At no time has the child been given any sense that she is 'misbehaving'. Linda does not impose any preconceptions of her own, or put limitations on what happens. Hannah herself is allowed to define the painting experience.

Red raspberries and blue trails

Of great significance is Hannah's use of distinctly different types of vocalisation to accompany equally distinct types of marking action and mark. Discontinuous, loud 'raspberries' are synchronised with vertical impacts and red blobs; quiet, continuous 'shhh's to accompany a continuous, slowly moving, blue line.

In this and other examples, she is exploring different types of equivalence (Arnheim, 1954, 1974) which are emerging from the same event. At one level of description, we can see this as the beginning of counting. She is counting her own movements and marks, and this will eventually lead to her use of the abstract numbering system. Another path of development is branching out from this episode which is based on her awareness that her movements and marks share characteristics with other objects and events.

A two-year-old has ideas about painting

This is the beginning of those associations between sound, movement and image we saw in earlier observations. She may have felt there was similarity between the sound of 'raspberries' and the sound and tactile sensations of a brush in squelchy paint, and between a soft 'shhh' and the sound of trailing bristles. She is exploring the idea that one action or image can echo, represent or be equivalent to another action or image. This is the basis for visual representation and expression. She is manipulating and playing not with objects alone, but with ideas.

Different kinds of realism

Although it is clear that Hannah is very pleased with her painting, some people might say that she will soon want to paint 'realistic' pictures and this is where development is taking her. But what is 'realistic' to a child changes with age and context. At various points in their lives children resist so-called 'advanced' systems because, far from making pictures more 'realistic' for them, these systems actually sacrifice understandings about their worlds which they feel to be important. For example, a table drawn in perspective loses its right-angular corners, and its rectangular shape is distorted. This may be part of the reason why, when children become interested in Euclidean or rigid geometry, they make drawings which preserve the structure of 'carpentered' objects. Although the notion of visual realism trips off the tongue even of art educators who should know better, it is a notoriously difficult term to define. As Dennis Atkinson has noted, children are often criticised for drawing things not as they really look; but how do things look 'really'? This criticism implies that the person assumes there is one true reality existing independently of the modes of representation we use to describe it. On the contrary, representation is not a copy of some absolute reality thought to exist independently of our human forms of representation, but is a human construction. In drawing, this means that visual reality (for want of a better word) takes shape, as it were, on the drawing surface. How that shape is made and what shapes are formed depends on the child's changing kinds of knowledge about the world and the priorities she has about what kind of information is necessary to be encoded within a given medium.

Drawing as an interplay of forces rather than the representation of objects

When obvious changes do occur in the way children represent the world, this partly reflects changes in their priorities about the type of information they feel it is essential to capture (Light, 1985). Children are harmed when they are forced to abandon these forms of expression and representation and are trained prematurely in narrow versions of drawing. The idea that the representation of objects is at the heart of drawing is completely wrong. As Arnheim has written, drawing is primarily an interplay of different forces (Arnheim, 1954, 1974).

It is helpful to study the different systems which artists have used in different places around the world and at different times. The Chinese, for example, were acquainted with the depiction of three-dimensional form as early as the seventh century but chose not to use it because they thought it was unsuitable for the aims of their painting. They were not thinking of the painting as a 'window' opening out onto a physical world but were trying to achieve a transcendental space (Sullivan, 1973; Edgerton, 1980). Indian painting often uses the vertical oblique projection system, in which plan views (for example, of carpets) are shown simultaneously with side elevations (of people and other objects). Vertical oblique and other systems are combined in Cubist painting and some postmodern art uses a multiplicity of symbol and signs, some of which are not linked to the visible world at all. It is a tragic irony that teachers who profess to be 'multicultural' and 'antiracist' (or even 'postmodern') while deifying artworks from other cultures, reveal their total lack of understanding by condemning the exact same systems as used by their pupils (see also Atkinson, 2002 forthcoming).

Although adult artists are different from children in that they have greater control over a range of representational systems, nevertheless young children also choose from a range of options available. As Hannah grows, she does not merely abandon these in favour of more advanced ones, rather they become reworked at new levels, transformed by revolutions in her thinking and integrated in more complex systems (Athey, 1990; Wolf, 1989). Modern and post-modern artists have admired children's art precisely for what they feel is its clarity of vision, as opposed to a photographic or linear perspective paradigm. Yet, even perspective drawing too, if understood properly, incorporates those early understandings about time, space and movement formed in infancy. Ben's case study is just one example.

Summary

In this book I have described the origin and development of children's use and organisation of visual media. I have argued that this is a continuum which exhibits semantic and organisational characteristics at every level, that is, it has structure and meaning all the way through. This is true of the outset of representation, during the period when, according to popular wisdom and to any number of other accounts, children are supposed to be mindlessly 'scribbling'. The fact that, in this book, the beginning of representation is so fundamentally different from other accounts has implications for the way we understand and provide for later education – and not just art education.

I have argued that drawing and painting can play a central role in the development of thinking and feeling. When children draw and paint they move through an important sequence of thinking and feeling. We have seen that there is an important mathematical aspect and that language is involved. Drawing and painting extend language, if adults talk intelligently with children about their drawings and paintings. Language organises drawing, and it might be that all representation owes much to the syntax of language. In fact, I have suggested that drawing and painting are part of an entire family of expressive and representational ways or 'modes' generated in infancy which are integrated to help the child form descriptions of their worlds.

We have seen that, as children grow older, their drawing changes. This is due to changes in their priorities about essential information to be encoded in a drawing (Light, 1985). These changes may be prompted by revolutions occurring periodically in the child's thinking. When children struggle to show more of the truth about their worlds, they produce drawings which may look strange to some adults. However, it is a mistake to measure these against a limited notion of visual realism and evaluate them in terms of supposed deficits. Even if new, electronic media are used, this in itself will not make a paradigm shift. The physical blackboard is simply replaced by an electronic one. The 'virtually real' merely replaces older paradigms of 'correct' representations. Children's drawings are frequently the result of combinations of different types of knowledge encoded in systems about which we still know little. It is our responsibility to decode these systems in order to help children understand how their lives and their worlds are represented within them. The better we understand our representations of the world, the better we will be able to cope with our own futures.

References

Ahlberg, J. and A. (1981) *Peepo!* London: Kestrel Books.

Allott, R. (2001) *The Natural Origin of Language: Vision, Action, Language*. Knebworth: Able Publishing.

Arnheim, R. (1954, 1974 2nd edn.) *Art and Visual Perception: The Psychology of the Creative Eye*. Berkeley: University of California Press.

Athey, C. (1977) Humour in children related to Piaget's theory of intellectual development, in A.J. Chapman and H.C. Foot (eds), *It's a Funny Thing, Humour*. Oxford: Pergamon Press.

Athey, C. (1990) *Extending Thought in Young Children: A Parent–Teacher Partnership*. London: Paul Chapman Publishing.

Atkinson, D. (2002 forthcoming) *Art Education: Identity and Practice*. Amsterdam: Kluwer Academic.

Awdry, W.V. (1997) *Thomas the Tank Engine: The Complete Collection*. New York: Random House.

Bartholomew, L. and Bruce, T. (1993) *Getting to Know You: A Guide to Record Keeping in Early Childhood Education*. London: Hodder and Stoughton.

Berefelt, G. (1987) Sex differences in scribbles of toddlers: graphic activity of 18 month old children. *Scandinavian Journal of Educational Research*, 31, pp. 23–30.

Berliner, D.C. and Biddle, B.J. (1995) *The Manufactured Crisis: Myths, Fraud, and Attack on America's Public Schools*. New York: Addison Wesley.

Bettelheim, B. (1987) *A Good Enough Parent*. London: Thames & Hudson.

Bickerton, D. (1981) *The Roots of Language*. Ann Arbor: Karoma Publishing.

Blenkin, G.M. and Kelly, A.V. (eds) (1996) *Early Childhood Education: A Developmental Curriculum*. (2nd edn.) London: Paul Chapman Publishing.

Bower, T.G.R. (1974, 1982 2nd edn.) *Development in Infancy*. San Francisco: Freeman.

Bremner, J.G. (1985) Figural biases and young children's drawings, in N.H. Freeman and M.V. Cox (eds), *Visual Order: The Nature and Development of Pictorial Representation*, pp. 301–31. Cambridge: Cambridge University Press.

Brown, T. (1997) Collaboration: life and death in the aesthetic zone. *Robert Rauschenberg: A Retrospective*. New York: Guggenheim Museum.

Bruce, T. (1987) *Early Childhood Education*. London: Hodder and Stoughton.

Bruce, T. (1991) *Time to Play in Early Childhood Education*. London: Hodder and Stoughton.

Bruner, J. (1990) Keynote paper. IVth European Conference on Developmental Psychology, University of Stirling, Scotland.

Bruner, J.S. (1964) The course of cognitive growth. *American Psychologist*, 19, pp. 1–15.

Burton, E. (1997) Artificial innocence: interactions between the study of children's drawing and artificial intelligence. *Leonardo*, 30 (4), pp. 301–9.

Button, V. and Esche, E. (2000) *Intelligence: New British Art 2000*. London: Tate Gallery.

Chafe, W. (1994) *Discourse, Consciousness and Time: The Flow and Displacement of Conscious Experience in Speaking and Writing.* Chicago: University of Chicago Press.

Chan, R. and Matthews, J. (2002a) Trajectory and impact: the representation of the terrorist suicide plane crashes in the U.S.A. in the drawings of 2 to 3 year olds in Singapore. Unpublished research study. Visual and Performing Arts, National Institute of Education, Nanyang Technological University, Singapore.

Chan, R. and Matthews, J. (2002b) Two-year-olds making movies: how children use digital movie videocameras. Unpublished research study. Visual and Performing Arts, National Institute of Education, Nanyang Technological University, Singapore.

Chomsky, N. (1966) *Cartesian Linguistics: A Chapter in the History of Rationalist Thought.* New York: Harper and Row.

Chomsky, N. (1994) *Language and Thought.* Wakefield, RI: Moyer Bell.

Chomsky, N. (1997) *Rules and Representation.* Cambridge: Cambridge University Press.

Condon, W. (1975) Speech makes babies move, in R. Lewin (ed.), *Child Alive*, pp. 81–90. London: Temple Smith.

Costall, A. (1993) Beyond linear perspective: a Cubist manifesto for visual science. *Image and Image Computing*, 11 (6), July/August, pp. 334–41.

Costall, A. (1995) The myth of the sensory core: the traditional versus the ecological approach to children's drawings, in C. Lange-Kuttner and G.V. Thomas (eds), *Drawing and Looking: Theoretical Approaches to Pictorial Representation in Children*, Hemel Hempstead and New York: Harvester Wheatsheaf.

Costall, A. (2001) Introduction and notes to G.H. Luquet's *Children's Drawings ('Le Dessin Enfantin')*, translation and commentary by A. Costall. London and New York: Free Association Books.

Cox, M. (1992) *Children's Drawing.* Harmondsworth: Penguin.

Cox, M. (1993) *Children's Drawings of the Human Figure.* Hillsdale, NJ: Lawrence Erlbaum Associates.

Cox, M. (1997) *Drawings of People by the Under-5's.* London: Falmer Press.

Cox, M.V., Cooke, G. and Griffin, D. (1995) Teaching children to draw in the infants school. *Journal of Art & Design Education*, 14, pp. 153–63.

Darwin, C. (1859) *Origin of Species.* Ware: Wordsworth Classics.

Davies, M. (2003) *Movement and Dance in Early Childhood.* (2nd edn.) London: Paul Chapman Publishing.

De Villiers, P.A. and de Villiers, J.G. (1979) *Early Language.* London: Fontana.

Duthie, R.K. (1985) The adolescent's point of view: studies of form in confliction, in N.H. Freeman and M.V. Cox (eds), *Visual Order: the Nature and Development of Pictorial Representation*, pp. 101–120. Cambridge: Cambridge University Press.

Easthope, A. (1999) *The Unconscious.* London: Routledge.

Edelman, G.M. (1987) Neural Darwinism. New York: Basic Books.

Edgerton, S.Y. (1980) The Renaissance artist as quantifier, in M.A. Hagen (ed.), *The Perception of Pictures, Vol. 1, Alberti's Window*, pp. 179–212. New York: Academic Press.

Eisner, E. (1997) Keynote paper on visual arts education, presented at the International Conference on 'The Arts and Education in Hong Kong': An International Symposium, Hong Kong Convention Centre, Lyric Theatre, Academy for Performing Arts, 20–22 March.

Eliot, L. (1999) *Early Intelligence: How the Brain and Mind Develop in the First Five Years of Life.* London: Penguin.

Fenson, L. (1985) The transition from construction to sketching in children's drawing, in N.H. Freeman and M.V. Cox (eds), *Visual Order: The Nature and Development of Pictorial Representation*, pp. 374–84. Cambridge: Cambridge University Press.

Ferreiro, E. and Teberowsky, A. (1982) *Literacy Before Schooling.* Oxford: Heinemann Educational.

Freeman, N. (1980) *Strategies of Representation in Young Children.* London: Academic Press.

Freeman, N.H. and Cox, M.V. (eds) (1985) *Visual Order: The Nature and Development of Pictorial Representation.* Cambridge: Cambridge University Press.

Freire, P. (2000) *Pedagogy of the Heart.* New York: Continuum Books.

Freud, S. (1915–17) *A General Introduction to Psychoanalysis (28 Lectures to Laypersons)*. London: Penguin.

Fucigna, C. (1983) Research proposal: M.A. Thesis. Tufts University MA.

Furth, H.G. (1969) *Piaget and Knowledge*. New Jersey: Prentice Hall.

Gardner, H. (1985) *Frames of Mind: The Theory of Multiple Intelligences*. London: Paladin.

Gardner, H. (1997) Keynote speech for *7th International Conference on Thinking*. Singapore 1–6 June.

Gesell, A. (1946) The ontogenesis of infant behaviour, in L. Carmichael (ed.), *Manual of Child Psychology*, pp. 295–331. New York: Wiley.

Gibson, J. (1966) *The Senses Considered as Perceptual Systems*. Boston: Houghton Mifflin.

Gibson, J.J. and Yonas, P. (1968) A new theory of scribbling and drawing in children, in H. Levin, E.J. Gibson and J.J. Gibson (eds), *The Analysis of Reading Skills*. Washington, DC: US Dept of Health, Education and Welfare, Office of Education.

Gibson, K.R. and Ingold, T. (1995) *Tools, Language and Cognition in Human Evolution*. Cambridge: Cambridge University Press.

Golomb, C. (1974) *Young Children's Sculpture and Drawing: A Study in Representational Development*. Cambridge, MA: Harvard University Press.

Golomb, C. (1992) *The Child's Creation of a Pictorial World*. Berkeley: University of California Press.

Golomb, C. (1993) Art and the young child: Another look at the developmental question. *Visual Arts Research*, 19, (1) pp. 1–16.

Gray, H. (1978) Learning to take an object from the mother, in A. Lock (ed.), *Action, Gesture and Symbol: The Emergence of Language*, pp. 159–183. London: Academic Press.

Harris, P. (1989) *Children and Emotion*. Oxford: Basil Blackwell.

Hohmann, M., Banet, B. and Weikart, D.P. (1979) *Young Children in Action*. Michigan: High/Scope Press.

Karmiloff-Smith, A. (1990) Constraints on representational change: evidence from children's drawing. *Cognition*, 34, pp. 57–83.

Kellogg, R. (1969) *Analyzing Children's Art*. Palo Alto, CA: National Press Books.

Kelly, A.V. (1990) *The National Curriculum: A Critical Review*. London: Paul Chapman Publishing.

Kindler, A. (1997a) Paper prepared for presentation at the INSEA International Conference: Our Futures in Design, Glasgow, 10–15 July.

Kindler, A. (ed.) (1997b) *Child Development in Art*. Reston, VA: National Art Education Association.

Kindler, A., Eisner, E. and Day, M. (eds) (2003) *Learning in the Visual Arts: Handbook of Research and Policy in Art Education*. Canada: University of British Columbia.

Kress, G. (1997) *Before Writing: Rethinking the Paths to Literacy*. London: Routledge.

Kunasegaran, S., Aljunied, M. and Matthews, J. (2002) *Developmental Approach to Understanding and Assessing Children's Drawing: A Drawing Development Assessment Resource for Primary School Art Teachers*. Singapore: Psychological Assessment and Research Branch, Ministry of Education.

Light, P. (1985) The development of view-specific representation considered from a socio-cognitive standpoint, in N.H. Freeman and M.V. Cox (eds), *Visual Order: The Nature and Development of Pictorial Representation*. Cambridge: Cambridge University Press.

Lorenz, K. (1996) *The Natural Science of the Human Species: An Introduction to Comparative Behavioural Research (The Russian Manuscript, 1944–1948)*. Cambridge, MA: MIT Press.

Lowenfeld, V. and Brittain, W.L. (1970) *Creative and Mental Growth*. New York: Macmillan.

Luquet, G.H. (1927) *Children's Drawings ('Le Dessin Enfantin')*, translation and commentary by A. Costall (2001). London and New York: Free Association Books.

Ma Ying, J. and Leong, W.Y.J. (2002) *The Art of Childhood and Adolescence: The Construction of Meaning: Exhibition Catalogue*. Visual and Performing Arts, National Institute of Education, Nanyang Technological University, Singapore.

Marr, D. (1982) *Vision: A Computational Investigation into Human Representation and Processing of Visual Information*. San Francisco: Freeman.

Matthews, J. (1983) Children drawing: are young children really scribbling? Paper presented at British Psychological Society's International Conference on 'Psychology and the Arts', University of Cardiff.

Matthews, J. (1984) Children drawing: are young children really scribbling? *Early Child Development and Care*, 18, pp. 1–39.

Matthews, J. (1992) The genesis of aesthetic sensibility, in D. Thistlewood (ed.), *Drawing, Art and Development*. London: NSEAD and Longman.

Matthews, J. (1994 Ist edn.) *Helping Children to Draw and Paint in Early Childhood: Children and Visual Representation*, 0–8 Series, London: Hodder and Stoughton.

Matthews, J. (1999) *The Art of Childhood and Adolescence: The Construction of Meaning*. London: Falmer Press.

Matthews, J. (2000a) The conversational structure of young children's use of visual media, in A. Brown (ed.), *English in SE Asia 99*, pp. 119–130. Singapore: National Institute of Education and Prentice Hall.

Matthews, J. (2000b) Within the picture: reconsidering intellectual and visual realism in children's drawing. A paper prepared for 'II International Congress in Children's Art', 27, 28 and 29 September, Madrid: University of Madrid.

Matthews, J. (2001a) Children drawing attention: studies from Singapore. *Visual Arts Research*, 27 (1) pp. 13–45. USA: University of Illinois.

Matthews, J. (2001b) Visual literacy: let children act naturally. *Five to Seven*, August. pp. 27–34.

Matthews, J. (2001c) Taking the toys from the boys: the suppression of male symbolisation in early years' education. Unpublished paper.

Matthews, J. (2002 in press) The art of infancy, in A. Kindler, E. Eisner and M. Day (eds), *Learning in the Visual Arts: Handbook of Research and Policy in Art Education*. Canada: University of British Columbia.

Matthews, J. (2003) *Large Glass of Water*. Underwater performance at 'The Art Gallery', Visual & Performing Arts, National Institute of Education, Nanyang Technological University, Singapore, 30 January 2003.

Matthews, J. and Jessel, J. (1993a) Very young children and electronic paint: the beginnings of drawing with traditional media and computer paintbox (shortened version), *Early Years*, Spring, 13 (2), pp. 15–22.

Matthews, J. and Jessel, J. (1993b) Very young children use electronic paint: a study of the beginnings of drawing with traditional media and computer paintbox (original version), *Visual Arts Research*, Spring, 19 (1), Issue 37, pp. 47–62.

Meadows, S. (1991) The development of writing, in P. Light, S. Sheldon and M. Woodhead (eds), *Learning to Think*, pp. 175–84. London: Routledge.

Michotte, A. (1963) *The Perception of Causality*. London: Methuen.

Monty Python's (1979) *Life of Brian*. (written by Graham Chapman) Criterion Collection. www. Amazon.com

Nasar, S. (2002) *A Beautiful Mind. The Life of Mathematical Genius and Nobel Laureate John Nash*. London: Simon & Schuster.

Petitto, L. (1987) Gestures and Language in Apes and Children. A talk given at the Medical Research Council's Cognitive Development Unit, London, 28 May.

Phillips, W.A., Hobbs, S.B. and Pratt, F.R. (1978) Intellectual realism in children's drawings of cubes. *Cognition*, 6, pp. 15–33.

Piaget, J. (1951) *Play, Dreams and Imitation in Childhood*. London: Routledge and Kegan Paul.

Piaget, J. and Inhelder, B. (1956) *The Child's Conception of Space*. London: Routledge and Kegan Paul.

Pietronigro, F. (2000) Research project number 33: Investigating the Creative Process in a Microgravity Environment. *Leonardo*, 33 (3) pp. 169–77.

Pinker, S. (1994) *The Language Instinct*. London: Penguin.

Piscitelli, B. (2001) Re-Reading Art for the Child under Seven. Seminar paper: School of Early Childhood, Centre for Applied Studies in Early Childhood, Queensland University of Technology, Brisbane, Australia.

Ranson, S. (1984) Towards a tertiary tripartism: new codes of social control and the 17+, cited in B. Simon, *Bending the Rules: The Baker 'Reform' of Education*. pp. 42–3. London: Lawrence and Wishart.

Rawson, P. (1982) Lecture at Goldsmiths School of Art, London: University of London.

Reddy, V. (1991) Playing with others' expectation: teasing and mucking about in the first year, in A. Whiten (ed.), *Natural Theories of Mind*, pp. 143–58. London: Blackwell.

Richards, M. (1980) *Infancy: World of the Newborn*. London: Harper Row.

Rose, B. (1992) *Allegories of Modernism: Contemporary Drawing*. New York: Museum of Modern Art.

Rush, M. (1999) *New Media in Late 20th-Century Art*. London: Thames & Hudson.

Selfe, L. (1977) *Nadia: A Case of Extraordinary Drawing Ability in an Autistic Child*. London: Academic Press.

Seow, A. and Matthews, J. (2000) *Daniel: A Case Study of an Autistic Child's Drawing: What can Drawings of an Autistic Child Teach Us about Development and Representation?* Unpublished Academic Exercise, Visual and Performing Arts, National Institute of Education, Nanyang Technological University, Singapore.

Simon, B. (1988) *Bending the Rules: The Baker 'Reform' of Education*. London: Lawrence and Wishart.

Smith, N.R. (1979) Developmental origins of structural variations in symbol form, in N.R. Smith and M.B. Franklin (eds.), *Symbolic Functioning in Childhood*, pp. 11–26. Hillsdale, NJ: Lawrence Erlbaum Associates.

Smith, N.R. (1983) *Experience and Art: Teaching Children to Paint*. New York: Teachers College Press.

Spelke, E.S. (1985) Perception of unity, persistence and identity: thoughts on infants' conceptions of objects, in J. Mehler and R. Fox (eds), *Neonate Cognition: Beyond the Blooming, Buzzing Confusion*. Hillsdale, NJ: Lawrence Erlbaum Associates.

Spelke, E.S. (1990) Origins of visual knowledge, in D.N. Osherson, S.M. Kosslyn and J.M. Hollerbach (eds), *An Invitation to Cognitive Science: Visual Cognition and Action*, pp. 99–128. Cambridge, MA: MIT Press.

Stern, D. (1977) *The First Relationship: Infant and Mother*. Glasgow: Fontana.

Stetsenko, A. (1995) The psychological function of children's drawing: a Vygotskian perspective, in C. Lange-Kuttner and G.V. Thomas (eds), *Drawing and Looking: Theoretical Approaches to Pictorial Representation in Children*, pp. 147–158. London and New York: Harvester Wheatsheaf.

Sullivan, M. (1973) *The Meeting of Eastern and Western Art from 16th Century to Present Day*. London: Thames & Hudson.

Sumsion, J. (1999) James' story: A decade in the life of a male early childhood professional. *Early Child Development and Care*, 159, pp. 5–16.

Tarr, P. (1990) More than movement: scribbling reassessed. *Visual Arts Research*, 16 (1), Issue 31, pp. 83–9.

Temple, A.T., Nathan, R.G. and Burris, N.A. (1982) *The Beginnings of Writing*. Boston: Allyn and Bacon.

Thelen, E. and Smith, L.B. (1994) *A Dynamic Systems Approach to the Development of Cognition and Action*. Cambridge, MA: MIT Press.

Thelen, E., Schoner, G., Scheier, C. and Smith, L.B. (2000) The dynamics of embodiment: a field theory of infant perseverative reaching. Behavioural and Brain Sciences 24 (1). Preprint on internet: www.cogsci.soton.ac.uk/bbs/Archive/bbs.thelen.html

Thomas, G.V. and Silk, A.M.J. (1990) *An Introduction to the Psychology of Children's drawings*. London and New York: Harvester Wheatsheaf.

Tormey, J. and Whale, G. (2002) On drawing, visual language and the pictorial image: an interview with John Willats. TRACEY (www.tracey.lboro.ac.uk) Electronic Journal on Contemporary Drawing Research and Practice.

Trevarthen, C. (1975) Early attempts at speech, in R. Lewin (ed.), *Child Alive*, pp. 62–80. London: Temple Smith.

Trevarthen, C. (1980) The foundations of intersubjectivity: the development of interpersonal and cooperative understanding in infants, in D. Olson (ed.), *The Social Foundations of Language and Thought: Essays in Honour of J.S. Bruner*, pp. 316–42. New York: W.W. Norton.

Trevarthen, C. (1984) How control of movement develops, in H.T.A. Whiting (ed.), *Human Motor Actions – Bernstein Reassessed*, pp. 223–59. Amsterdam: Elsevier Science Publishers.

Trevarthen, C. (1988) Human communication is emotional as well as cognitive – from the start. A talk given at the Medical Research Council's Cognitive Development Unit, Euston, London, 23 June.

Trevarthen, C. (1995) Mother and baby – seeing artfully eye to eye, in R. Gregory, J. Harris, P. Heard and D. Rose (eds), *The Artful Eye*, pp. 157–200. Oxford: Oxford University Press.

Trevarthen, C. and Grant, F. (1979) Infant play and the creation of culture. *New Scientist*, February, pp. 566–9.

Trevarthen, C. and Hubley, P. (1978) Secondary intersubjectivity: confidence, confiding and acts of meaning in the first year, in A. Locke (ed.), *Action, Gesture and Symbol: The Emergence of Language*, pp. 183–229. London: Academic Press.

Van Sommers, P. (1984) *Drawing and Cognition: Descriptive and Experimental Studies in Graphic Production*. Cambridge: Cambridge University Press.

Vygotsky, L.S. (1966) Play and its role in the mental development of the child. *Soviet Psychology*, 12 (6), pp. 62–76.

Vygotsky, L.S. (1986) *Thought and Language*. Cambridge, MA: MIT Press.

Wartofsky, M.W. (1980) Visual scenarios: the role of representation in visual perception, in M.A. Hagen (ed.), *The Perception of Pictures*, Vol. 2, pp. 131–52. New York and London: Academic Press.

Whale, G. (2002) Why use computers to make drawings? Conference paper. *Creativity and Cognition 2002 Conference*. Loughborough University School of Art and Design.

White, B.L., Castle, P. and Held, R. (1964) Observations on the development of visually directed teaching, *Child Development*, 35, pp. 349–64.

White, M. and Stevenson, C. (1997) *Drawing on the Art of Children: An Historical Perspective of Children's Art in the Twentieth Century*. Catalogue for Exhibition, 11 September–6 October, Macquarie University Library.

Whitehead, M. (1990) *Early Literacy*. London: Paul Chapman Publishing.

Willats, J. (1984) Getting the picture to look right as well as be right: the interaction between production and perception as a mechanism of development, in W.R. Crozier and A.J. Chapman (eds), *Cognitive Processes in the Perception of Art*. Amsterdam: North Holland.

Willats, J. (1985) Drawing systems revisited: the role of denotational systems in children's figure drawings, in N.H. Freeman and M.V. Cox (eds), *Visual Order: The Nature and Development of Pictorial Representation*, pp. 78–100. Cambridge: Cambridge University Press.

Willats, J. (1992) The representation of extendedness in children's drawings of sticks and discs, in *Child Development*, 63, pp. 692–710.

Willats, J. (1997) *Art and Representation: New Principles in the Analysis of Pictures*. Princeton, NJ: Princeton University Press.

Wilson, B. (1997) Types of child art and alternative developmental accounts: interpreting the interpreters. *Human Development*, 40 (3), B. Rogoff (ed.), Karger: Basel, pp.155–168.

Wilson, B. (2000) Keynote paper, 2000 Asia-Pacific Art Education Conference, Regional Experiences and Prospects in the New Century, Hong Kong Institute of Education, Hong Kong, 28–31 December.

Wilson, B. and Wilson, M. (1985) The artistic tower of Babel: inextricable links between culture and graphic development. *Visual Arts Research*, 11, pp. 90–104.

Winner, E. (1989) How can Chinese children draw so well? *Journal of Aesthetics Education*, 22, pp. 17–34.

Winnicott, D. (1971) *Playing and Reality*. London: Tavistock.

Wolf, D. (1984) Repertoire, style and format: notions worth borrowing from children's play, in P.K. Smith (ed.), *Play in Animals and Humans*, pp. 175–93. Oxford: Blackwell.

Wolf, D. (1989) Artistic learning as a conversation, in D. Hargreaves (ed.), *Children and the Arts*, pp. 23–39. Milton Keynes: Open University Press.

Wolf, D. and Fucigna, C. (1983) Representation before picturing. Paper presented at the Symposium on Drawing Development, British Psychological Society International Conference on Psychology and the Arts, University of Cardiff, Wales.

Wolf, D. and Perry, M.D. (1988) From endpoints to repertoires: some new conclusions about drawing development. *Journal of Aesthetic Education*, 2 (1), Spring, pp. 17–34.

Zhensun, Z. and Low, A. (1991) *A Young Painter: The Life and Paintings of Wang Yani – China's Extraordinary Young Artist*. New York: Scholastic Inc.

Index

DATE DUE